Baby Things to Make

by Regina Nast

Table of Contents

Publishers: Bill and Helen Fisher
Executive Editor: Rick Bailey
Editorial Director: Randy Summerlin
Editor: Judith Schuler
Art Director: Don Burton
Book Design: Dana Martin
Photography: Richard Nast
Illustrations: Cynthia Johnoff

HPBooks®
P.O. Box 5367
Tucson, Arizona 85703
(602) 888-2150
ISBN: 0-89586-229-8
Library of Congress Catalog Card Number: 83-81885
© 1983 Fisher Publishing, Inc.
Printed in U.S.A.

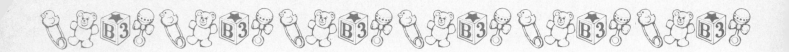

Welcoming Baby

This book offers you a variety of baby-gift ideas to make. It will also help you if you're an expectant parent who is looking for a single source of basic necessities. Different sections contain everything from padded, reversible crib sheets to unique ways of handling birth announcements.

Along with layette items for the nursery and infant-toddler clothing, there are quilts, wall hangings, mobiles, dolls, toys and many other useful, decorative items. In addition to a variety of projects, you will find different methods used to make them. Besides sewing, you will use techniques of appliqué, embroidery and quilting.

There are projects for making collages, shadow boxes, mobiles and corsages. There are simple woodworking projects, paper crafts, braiding, gluing, macramé and cartooning.

If you don't have expertise in crafts, you may be looking for a place to start. Projects in each section range in difficulty from easy to hard. It is often possible for a child to participate, enabling brothers or sisters to join in welcoming a new baby.

All the projects can be customized. Instead of trying to reproduce the projects shown in the photographs, try alternative suggestions. As you begin collecting your own materials, you'll come up with new combinations. As you create your own variations, one project will lead to another.

These projects all relate to baby, but most can be used for other things as well. The *Shower Wreath*, page 127, and *Shower Mobile*, page 115, can be adapted for a wedding. The *Covered Albums*, page 153, and *Covered Frames*, page 150, can be used for birthdays and anniversaries. The *Welcome-Baby Wreath*, page 140, can help children develop reading and writing skills. Older children might enjoy making the *T-Shirt Mobile*, page 124. The *Nursery Laundry Bag*, page 47, *Hanging Diaper Stacker*, page 48, and *Braided Rocker Cover*, page 52, can be adapted to other household purposes.

A word of caution. *Safety* is always a concern when making crafts. When making things for babies, special precautions must be taken. Securely stitch buttons and other small attachments on clothing, dolls and toys. Remove plastic ends from shoelaces. To avoid splinters and sharp edges on wood toys, thoroughly sand surfaces. Use only non-toxic paint for objects baby will handle. Follow directions on page 114 for safely hanging mobiles.

When making crafts with small children, supervise their use of scissors, sewing equipment, glue and felt-tip pens. Protect your work area from spills and other accidents with some type of cover. Pay special attention to any project you may be working on for other safety precautions.

Construction Terms, Techniques and Equipment

When reading the instructions on how to make different projects, you will find many references to these pages. In this section you will find explanations of procedures. Read all instructions for a particular project *before* you begin. You might want to make a trial version of the project before investing time and money in it. For more detailed information on sewing techniques, see HPBooks' *Sewing: The Complete Guide.*

APPLIQUÉ

Appliqué is the method of decorating fabric by stitching or fusing a shaped piece of fabric on it. Shapes can be simple, consisting of one piece. They can also be more complex with multiple pieces and shapes, such as the dachshund on the *Bumper Pads,* page 36. Appliqués may be purchased or made at home. You may want to make your own appliqué but don't want to design it. Work with a child's drawing or a line drawing from a coloring book.

Directions that follow are for traditional stitching. Appliqués may also be fused. See the *Appliquéd Training Pants,* page 81. When possible, use embroidery hoops for hand-stitching appliqué work.

Choose fabrics of similar weight that do not ravel. To keep loosely woven fabric from raveling, back it with fusible interfacing. Felt is the easiest fabric to appliqué because edges do not need to be hemmed. Be-Transfer the design to the wrong-side of the fabric. Leave a 1/4-inch seam allowance. Flip the pattern over, if necessary, to match other pattern pieces. Cut out pattern pieces. Clip curves and angled areas outside the line. See illustration below.

Clip curves and angled areas.

Hand Appliqué—Apply iron-on interfacing to the wrong-side of the fabric. This prevents fraying. Turn raw edges to the wrong-side along the outline of the appliqué. Stitch in place with a temporary basting-stitch or permanent invisible-stitch, page 13. Press.

Determine the position of the appliqué before stitching it to the garment or project. Baste it on the background in the order the appliqués are to be sewn. Hand-stitch appliqués with an invisible- or slip-stitch if you don't want stitches to show. Use a thread compatible with the weight of the fabric. For more-decorative stitching, use embroidery thread and a buttonhole- or running-stitch. See page 9 for information on *Embroidery Stitches.*

Machine Appliqué—Cut out the appliqué. To keep the appliqué from slipping and puckering while stitching, apply fusible interfacing to the appliqué fabric. You can also use tissue paper on the back of the appliqué to keep it from sticking. Pin the design on the background, and tack it in place. Machine-stitch around the outline with a running-stitch. Sew over the running-stitch with a short-length, medium-to-wide zigzag-stitch. Cut away excess fabric outside the stitching line.

Stuffing Appliqués—To create dimension, appliqués can be stuffed with batting. You can do this two ways, depending on whether the wrong-side of the backing is going to be seen. If the backing is visible, add the appliqué as described on page 50. Leave a 1- to 1-1/2-inch opening at the edge. Insert the batting with a chopstick or other stuffing tool, page 18. Arrange batting so the appliqué is evenly padded. Stitch the opening closed.

If the backing does not show, as with the *Cloth Books,* page 102, or the *Nursery Laundry Bag,* page 47, top-stitch the appliqué in position. Carefully separate layers so the appliqué is not cut. Basting stitches on a quilt. Slash the backing fabric under the appliqué. Make the slash 1 to 1-1/2 inches or as wide as necessary to keep from interfering with top-stitching. Stuff the appliqué from the back opening. Stitch the opening closed.

BASTING QUILTS

Basting will keep the backing, batting and front pieces from shifting during quilting. See information on *Embroidery Stitches,* page 9. It will help make the layers as flat as possible. Begin the layering process by basting. The more rows you baste, the more stable your layers will be. Quilting will also be smoother.

Before basting, pin the three layers together with straight pins in four lines. Start at the center and work horizontally on either side to make the first line. Work vertically on the second line, then diagonally, forming an X.

Use a single strand of thread in a contrasting color and a long, thin needle. See page 21 for information on *Needles.* Push the needle through all three layers. Leave a 2- to 3-inch tail on the thread for easy removal. Do not knot the thread. Start basting from the center and work out.

Begin with the diagonal lines and work from opposite sides.

Stitch to the horizontal line of pins, then to the vertical line. Again working from the center, run rows of basting stitches 5 inches apart horizontally and vertically. See illustration below.

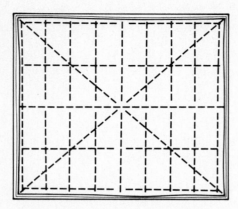

Baste 3 layers together in this manner. Start all basting lines from center out.

BIAS AND BINDING FOR PROJECTS

Bias Strips—Bias strips are bands of fabric cut at a 45° angle to the lengthwise or crosswise grain of the fabric. They are used to finish raw edges. Strips can be purchased or made from self-fabric. They usually show on the right- and wrong-side of the finished project.

Bands can be made as short strips, then joined, or made as continuous strips. Continuous strips are useful for a project needing larger amounts of bias, such as a quilt edge.

To make short bias strips, straighten the fabric and iron it along the lengthwise and crosswise grains. Fold fabric diagonally, with the fold representing the true grain. Keep the lengthwise grain parallel to the crosswise grain. If making bias from stretch fabric, cut fabric across the grain so it goes *with* the stretch.

With a colored pencil or fabric marker, mark lines parallel to the crosswise grain. Measure the distance between each length of bias

with a ruler. Make lines the desired width, plus a 1/4-inch seam allowance. Cut along the marked lines. See illustration below.

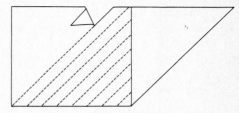

Lines parallel to crosswise grain

Cut away the triangular ends, then cut strips. To join bias strips, pin two strips together, with right-sides matching. Strips form a V-shape. See illustration below. Stitch, then press seams open, and press raw edges inward.

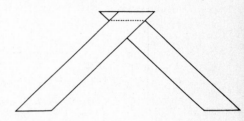

Joining bias strips

Bias strips can be made as single-fold or double-fold. A double-fold bias strip has extra strength for holding thicker edges, such as quilt edges. Single-fold bias strips are good for clothing items, like booties. The single-fold allows for a narrower, less-bulky finish. See illustration below.

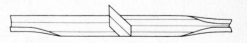

Single-fold bias   Double-fold bias

Continuous Bias—Cut a wide strip of true bias. On the wrong-side of the fabric, mark a bias line from one corner to another. Make parallel lines the required width and add 1/4 inch for seam allowances. Mark as many strips as needed. Trim the excess fabric, but don't cut the strips.

With right-sides together, fold the fabric into a tube. One strip extends beyond the edge on each side. See illustration below. Stitch a 1/4-inch seam, and press it open. Begin cutting at one end. Cut a line around the tube, beginning at the first line. Continue cutting in a spiral until you reach the other end.

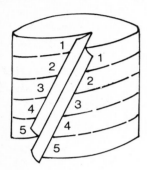

Continuous bias

Adding Binding—With right-sides together, open one fold of bias. Pin one edge of the bias to the edge of the garment, leaving ends open. To make binding fit curves, stretch binding around them.

Stitch binding 1/4 inch from the matched raw edges. At the ends of the binding, lap the second end over the first. Trim excess fabric, but leave a 1/4-inch seam allowance.

With right-sides facing, stitch the ends together. Turn binding to the inside over the raw edges. Turn under the raw edges and slip-stitch the binding to the seam line. For more information on adding binding, see *Mitering*, page 14.

BRAIDING THREE STRANDS

Divide material to be braided into three equal sections. Hold the center strand tautly. Begin weaving as close to the top as possible.

Cross the outside strand on the right over the center strand. The first center strand is now on the right. The first strand on the right

becomes the center strand. Take the strand on the left and make it the center strand by crossing it over the existing one.

Return to the right side. Cross over the center to the left side. Repeat this process of alternating sides and crossing over the center strand until the braid is the desired length. See illustration below.

Braiding with 3 strands

BUTTONHOLES

There are two types of buttonholes used on projects in this book. They are the *bound buttonhole* and *worked buttonhole*.

Bound Buttonholes—This type of buttonhole is used on the *Fitted Infant-Seat Cover*, page 40, and the *Car-Seat Cover*, page 38. It is supported by continuous bias.

Bound buttonholes give a professional look to garments and long-wearing use to projects. For the projects in this book, you will use the one-piece bound buttonhole. These buttonholes are made through fabric and interfacing only.

Cut a strip of fabric on the straight or bias grain. It should be 2 inches wider and 1 inch longer than the buttonhole. Bias pieces are preferable because fabric cut on the bias has stretch. This reduces the risk of fabric pieces pulling away and the buttonhole fraying.

Mark the center of each strip with tailor's chalk. Transfer size markings with tacking lines, and center the fabric strip over the buttonhole. Position right-sides together, and tack all around.

Machine-stitch along the lines

on the long sides. Each line must be exactly the same length. Stitch twice for strength. Tie thread ends on the wrong-side.

On the right-side, fold the edges of the binding toward the buttonhole center. Press one after the other. From the wrong-side, slash along the center of the binding between the stitching lines. Use small sharp scissors. Stop 1/4 inch from each end. Place a pin 1/4 inch from each end to prevent overcutting.

Do the same on the garment side. If the slash is too long, the triangles at either end are too small to handle. Buttonholes will be weak in these places.

From the ends of the slash, clip diagonally to each corner. Be careful not to cut any stitches. Remove tacking-stitches and push binding through the opening. Press away from the opening, then make an inverted pleat at both ends. Folds meet exactly in the center of the slit. Tack folds together.

With the right-side of the garment facing you, fold back the edge of the opening. This exposes a corner triangle. Machine-stitch across the base of the triangle using short stitches. Stitch each triangle twice. Carefully tie thread ends. Trim binding and catch-stitch edges to the interfacing.

To finish, pin and tack the facing to the garment through all layers of fabric and interfacing. Place pins across each end of the buttonhole to mark the size on the facing.

Make a slash on the facing between pins. Clip the center of each slash. Turn in the edges, and slip-stitch the facing to the buttonhole on the wrong-side. This makes an oval shape.

Hand-Sewn Buttonholes—These buttonholes are best for fine, dainty, lightweight fabrics. They are also good for baby garments and in some cases are stronger than bound buttonholes.

Badly sewn buttonholes that

are not level or stitched evenly are noticeable on a garment or project. Practice making buttonholes on a scrap of fabric first. See the *Buttonhole-stitch*, page 10.

Mark the buttonhole by placing a pin at either end. Slash along the *exact* center line. Pins prevent the slash from going too far. Remove pins. For extra strength, place a line of stitching in a rectangle 1/8 inch from the slit.

On fabrics that fray, overcast the edges of the slit. Stitch neatly or thick, lumpy stitching will show on the finished buttonhole.

Starting on the right-side, work buttonhole-stitches to the end of the first side. Use a 20-inch length of thread. If a longer thread is used, it may be difficult to manipulate. This causes thread to twist and knot.

Insert the needle in the slash from the right-side. Bring it out a little outside the stitching line. Bring the thread around under the point from the eye of the needle. Draw the needle through the fabric to form a knot at the edge of the slash.

Continue along the slit to one end. Stitch a fan-shape around the end. Continue in a buttonhole-stitch along the other side. Keep stitches even and close together to cover the cut edge. Do not pull knots too tight because this buckles the fabric edge.

Make several stitches across the end covering the last stitches to form a bar tack. Work buttonhole-stitches through the fabric and bar tack. Finish neatly and securely. If a straight effect is preferred, finish both ends in a bar tack. A fan-shape usually looks daintier.

Machine-Stitched Buttonholes— Machine-stitched buttonholes give a crisp, long-wearing finish. They are good for casual or semi-casual wear and projects. A sewing machine can make beautiful buttonholes. Set the machine accurately, and stitch slowly and carefully.

Machine-stitched buttonholes are especially suitable for long-wearing, washable baby clothes. They can be sewn on zigzag and running-stitch machines with a buttonhole attachment.

A buttonhole attachment has a set of templates in various sizes. A template is selected and inserted in the attachment. The templates are various sizes, in oval and key-hole shapes. Buttonholes are uniform in length.

Mark the length and placement of the buttonholes on the fabric. Use interfacing as close as possible to the fabric color. Follow instructions from your sewing-machine handbook. This gives the setting for length and width of the stitch required to make a satin-stitch. On some machines, buttonholes are worked automatically. Often the machine can stitch the buttonhole without the operator turning the fabric.

Make a test sample. As fabrics vary, so does the machine setting. Use the same number of fabric layers on the test sample as for the final buttonhole. When you set a satin-stitch, fabric runs through the machine without you having to move the fabric.

If the work requires pulling, the stitch has not been set correctly. This results in stitches piling up and a lumpy buttonhole.

Strong, neat buttonholes may be worked with the stitch not larger than a satin-stitch. A strong buttonhole can be made by running a strand of thread under the stitches while sewing. Most zigzag machines have an extra sewing foot for buttonholes that allows this.

Attach the facing and interfacing, and trace buttonhole markings. Stitch the buttonholes, following machine instructions. For strong buttonholes, stitch around a second time.

If machine-stitching, stitch the buttonhole, then slit material. If working by hand, slit the material first, then stitch around the slit with the buttonhole-stitch. Finish sides with bar tacks.

CUTTING

Accurate, precise cutting is necessary for any project. If you want clothes to fit well and projects to look nice, you must cut carefully. Use the correct equipment and take your time. See the *Equipment* list, page 19.

Preparing Pattern—Enlarge pattern pieces to the size you need, then cut them out. See page 12 for information on enlarging patterns. Some of the pattern pieces will be traced more than once. Decide how many pieces you need by referring to the pattern.

Layout—Pattern instructions indicate any special layout directions, including whether or not to fold the fabric. Fabric is usually folded lengthwise, with selvages matching along one edge. When cutting tiny baby clothes, which require smaller amounts of fabric, a partial lengthwise fold may work. A partial fold is made on the lengthwise grain with one selvage placed a measured distance from the fold. The rest of the fabric is a single layer.

You may find it more economical or practical to fold the fabric crosswise. Don't use this method for napped or one-way fabrics.

You can use a double lengthwise fold or combine folds. It depends on the pattern and the amount of fabric you have to work with. With the double fold, fabric is folded twice along the lengthwise grain. Use this method when front and back pieces are cut on the fold or when you have to work around an irregularity or crease in the fabric.

Combined folds can be made to fit pattern pieces on a smaller amount of fabric. Combining folds means fabric is folded in two different ways for the layout. Any combination of folds can be used. The normal procedure is to lay pattern pieces out for one part, cut off remaining fabric and fold again. Before cutting off the second section, measure to be sure you have enough fabric.

Cutting Fabric—Place pattern

pieces as close together as possible on the grain line. Pin along lengthwise fold lines. Too many pins may cause distortion of the fabric and make the grain inaccurate. Use only enough pins to secure pieces. Distortion can also result if pattern pieces are not pinned in the correct direction on the grain.

Before starting to cut, check your pattern layout to be sure you have all the pattern pieces. Practice with different layouts to make the best use of your fabric. Cut the correct number of pattern pieces. For some patterns, pieces need to be turned over as indicated.

Select the proper cutting tool, page 19. When cutting, keep fabric flat on the cutting surface. Bent-handled shears are easiest for doing this. Take long, firm strokes along straight edges, and short snips on curved areas.

Save fabric scraps—they can be used for making buttonholes or for testing fabric. Scraps can also be used for other things, especially projects using small pieces of fabric or patchwork. See the *Puff Quilt,* page 24.

Marking Fabric Pieces—After fabric is cut, before the pattern is removed, mark the fabric for dart, tuck and gathering lines. Mark pockets, fold lines and matching marks. Seam lines may also be marked. See page 20 for *Fabric-Marking Tools.*

DARTS
Darts are tapered folds of fabric stitched on the wrong-side of a fabric section. They control fullness and turn flat fabric into shapes. Darts are not usually needed for baby clothing, but are necessary for fitted baby-seat covers.

Carefully sew and press darts for a smooth, round effect. Placement and stitching of some darts may be part of the design.

Straight Dart—Transfer markings to the fabric with tailor's chalk or tailor's tacks. Fold fabric so the dart side markings match. Place the point of the dart on the fold. Put pins at right angles to the fold, and tack close to the stitching line. Try on and adjust for fit.

Machine-stitch along the stitching line. Start at the wide end, and taper to almost nothing at the point. Run the last two or three stitches along the fold at the point so puckers do not appear on the right-side.

Smooth the line of stitching between finger and thumb. Sew ends through stitches on the underside at the tapered point, and remove tacking.

Press on the wrong-side along each side of the stitching. Press the dart to one side over a curved surface. This helps retain shape and smoothness. Vertical darts are usually pressed toward the center of the garment. Horizontal darts are pressed down, so check pattern instructions. Deep darts on thick fabrics are trimmed, opened and pressed flat. Edges can be overcast.

EASING
Easing is a way to prevent puckering and gathering on the outside of fabric when two different lengths are sewn together. With right-sides together, pin the two fabrics at intervals. Keep the layer that is being eased on top. Baste fabric, then stitch. See illustration below.

Easing 2 fabrics together

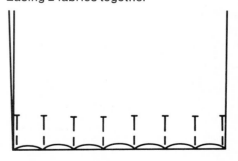

ELASTIC ADDED TO CASING
Make casing the width of the elastic, plus 1/4 inch. Turn the casing edge to the wrong-side, pin and press. Turn under raw edges and stitch with a hemming- or slip-stitch, page 14. Another way is to leave raw edges unturned and sew a zigzag-stitch with your sewing machine. This allows for greater give in the fabric. Leave a small opening in the casing.

Cut the piece of elastic the same length as the opening. To insert elastic, attach a safety pin to one end of it. Feed the pin and elastic through the casing.

Overlap elastic ends 1/2 inch and stitch twice. Ease the elastic inside the casing. Stitch the opening closed. For illustrated examples, see the *Sleepy Clown,* page 92, and *Party Dress,* page 74.

EMBROIDERY STITCHES
Back-Stitch—This is a strong hand-stitch that can be used in place of straight machine-stitching. Stitches look like machine-stitches on one side, yet overlap on the other.

With right-sides together, attach the thread and take one long running-stitch. Take a stitch back, and bring the needle out again a little way along the seam line. Repeat. See illustration below.

Back-stitch

Many sewing machines back-stitch. The resulting seam is elastic and strong. It is usually called a *triple seam.*

Basting—This stitch is important because it can make the difference between a beautiful finish and a messy one. There are times when it is not necessary to baste, but not often.

Basting is used to temporarily hold the garment or project together. It holds hems, seams and darts in position, ready for final stitching. It also marks construction details on the fabric.

Basting is used to identify certain sections of the garment or project, such as center-front lines or hemlines. It can also position items to be added to the garment such as zippers, braid and pockets. To make a basting-stitch, sew large running-stitches.

Blanket-Stitch—This stitch is used to finish raw edges, especially on blankets. It is also used on seams and to strengthen thread loops and bar tacks. It may be used as a simple decorative stitch. It can be worked from right to left or left to right.

Attach thread with one or two back-stitches. Push the needle in behind the fabric and through the loop. Keep the fabric edge toward you. Repeat. See illustration below.

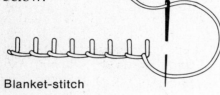

Blanket-stitch

Buttonhole-Stitch—The buttonhole-stitch is used to finish and strengthen raw edges, especially buttonholes. It is worked from left to right.

Attach thread with one or two back-stitches. Loop the thread behind the eye of the needle. With the needle behind the edge, push the needle point out over the loop of thread. Pull the needle through. Ease the thread up to form a knot on the edge. Make stitches close enough together to make a continuous row of knots along the edge. See illustration below.

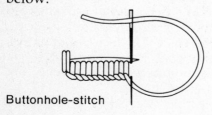

Buttonhole-stitch

Chain-Stitch—This is a decorative hand-embroidery stitch. Insert the needle in the right-side of the fabric. Hold the thread down

with your left thumb. Move the needle back to where the thread emerges. Bring out the needle and thread a short distance away. Bring the needle out over the loop. See illustration below.

Chain-stitch

Cross-Stitch—This stitch is a type of embroidery-stitch used in combination with other stitches. It is also used alone. See illustration below. Cross-stitch can be done

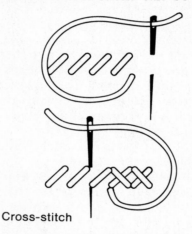

Cross-stitch

on almost any type of fabric, from gingham to canvas. Always begin cross-stitch in the following way, regardless of the background material.

On the center of your pattern, mark two intersecting lines. This divides the pattern into four parts so you can work your cross-stitch in sections.

To transfer the pattern to fabric, sew two long, intersecting basting-stitches that correspond to the lines drawn on your pattern. Make both lines an equal distance from the edges if you want your design centered. For your cross-stitch, begin counting checks or threads from these basting lines.

Gingham checks are great for a beginner. Each piece of gingham fabric has uniform squares of one

color and white. You can purchase gingham fabric with many different-size squares. If squares are even, any check fabric can be used. If you use fabric with small squares, your pattern will be reduced. Large squares are easier to work with, and the pattern is enlarged.

To do a cross-stitch on checks, make a cross-stitch in each fabric check that corresponds to a square from the pattern. Copy the pattern onto the fabric. Work square to square as you would for enlarging a pattern. See page 12 for information on enlarging a pattern.

Plain-weave fabric can be used for cross-stitch. Linen, monk's cloth or canvas are possible choices, as is any other plain weave with uniform threads large enough to count.

To cross-stitch on plain-weave fabric, count threads instead of checks. Do not mark the fabric, except for the center basting lines. Follow the pattern and mentally divide the plain weave into squares.

On the next page are cross-stitch patterns for numbers and the alphabet. Also included are other designs used in the *Shadow-Box Birth Announcement*, page 133.

Mount cross-stitch over batting before setting it in a frame. Trim the fabric about 1/2 inch larger on all sides than the board. Cut a thin piece of batting the same size as the board. Glue batting to the board with a small amount of spray adhesive.

Place the completed cross-stitch with its right-side down on a clean working surface. Center the board over it, with the batting-side facing the fabric. With a pencil, lightly trace the shape of the board on the wrong-side of the fabric.

Clip outside edges of the fabric about 1/8 inch from the traced line. Bring the edges to the wrong-side of the board, and glue them in place. See the *Covered Frames*, page 150, for this technique.

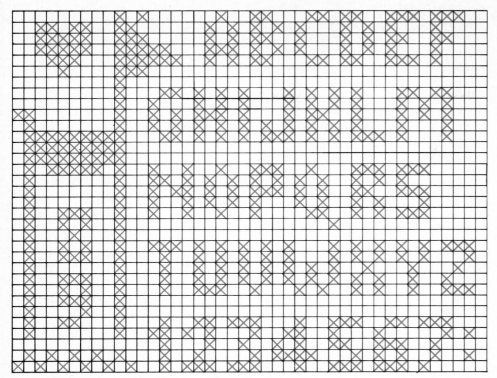

Cross-stitch patterns

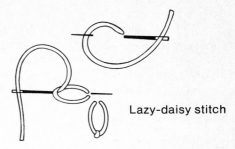

Lazy-daisy stitch

Feather-Stitch—This is another hand-embroidery stitch. Insert the needle to make a blanket-stitch, but slant the needle to the right. Put the thread to the left under the needle to make a blanket- or loop-stitch. Thread is slanted to the left. Repeat the process. See illustration below.

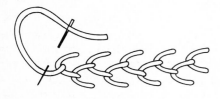

Feather-stitch

French Knot—This stitch is often used to make the center of embroidered flowers. Mark dots where knots should be. Pick up one or two threads of fabric. Wind the embroidery thread around the needle two or three times. Hold the thread down with your thumb, and pull the needle through. Insert the needle in the fabric close to the starting point. See illustration in next column.

French knot

Ladder-Stitch—This is two lines of blanket-stitches that face one another to form a ladder. First complete one line of stitching, then sew the second line of stitching. The ladder-stitch is often used to fill spaces of varying widths, as well as parallel lines. See illustration below.

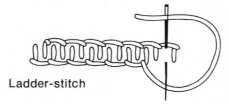

Ladder-stitch

Lazy-Daisy Stitch—This is a variation of the chain-stitch and is a detached chain-stitch. Groups of these stitches are often made together to form flowers in simple embroidery designs. See illustration in next column.

Overcasting—This is a quick way to finish raw edges by hand. Overcasting is often worked on a single layer of fabric. The thread is taken over the edge of the cloth all the way along. Stitches should be small and evenly spaced. Zigzag-stitches may be used on zigzag machines. Consult your sewing-machine handbook.

Overcasting can be used to join two finished edges or selvages. Move the needle from right to left, over the two edges. If tiny stitches are used, it is called a *whip-stitch*. Oversewing may also be done with the needle slanting so tiny, straight stitches are formed. See illustration below.

Overcasting

Running-Stitch—This is used when there is not much strain on a seam, and for easing and gathering. For seams, make stitches 1/16 to 1/8 inch long. For easing or gathering, stitches are 1/8 to 1/4 inch long.

Push the needle tip in and out of the fabric. Make small, regular stitches, evenly spaced, in straight or curved lines as required. Use a long, fine needle. Push it in and out for about six stitches before pulling the thread out. See illustration below. Running- and basting-stitches are the same. The basting-stitch is a larger stitch.

Running-stitch

Satin-Stitch—This is a decorative

stitch used in hand-embroidery and appliqué. Insert the needle at one edge of the design, then at the opposite edge. Return to the starting edge by passing the needle underneath the fabric. Make stitches close together and parallel. This stitch can be used to fill in a design of flowers, leaves and other decorations. It can also be made on a zigzag machine. See illustration below.

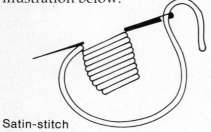

Satin-stitch

Tacking—Tacking-stitches are used as reinforcement at points of strain or to join areas not held together with seams. There are several kinds of tacking-stitches. The stitch used in this book for reinforcement is the *cross-stitch tack.* Follow directions for making the cross-stitch, page 10. Use one stitch or several, depending on how many are necessary.

The plain-stitch tack is used for joining areas not held together with seams, such as the puff sections of the *Welcome-Baby Wreath,* page 140. It is like an invisible- or plain hem-stitch, page 13, except stitches are farther apart.

Top-Stitching—Top-stitching is decorative stitching seen on the right-side of the fabric. Stitches can be machine-made or hand-sewn. A running-stitch is often used for top-stitching.

For more information of hand-stitches, see *Hem Stitches,* page 13.

ENLARGING PATTERNS

Some projects in this book must be enlarged before you begin making them. A graph simplifies the enlarging process. It lets you recreate the original shape a section at a time.

As you begin drawing, set aside your concept of the whole pattern, the shape of the girl in the example below. Concentrate on the shape and placement of the line within each individual square of the graph. This line is re-drawn on the correlating square of larger graph. As indicated in each project, patterns in this book are reduced to either one-half or one-quarter the original size.

Most paper can be used for enlarging. Tissue paper is the easiest to work with if you want to cut out the enlargement and use it as the pattern. It is also possible to make the enlargement on one type of paper, then trace the pattern on some other paper. For tissue paper, use the plain gift-wrapping type. You can also use 44-inch-wide tissue paper marked with 1-inch dots. If you are making your own graph, measure squares with a ruler, yardstick or other tool that has a straight edge.

Simplify marking the new graph from square to square with the pattern shape. Begin by numbering the squares horizontally and vertically on both the reduced pattern and the enlarged graph. See illustration below.

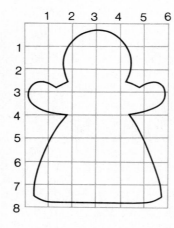

Numbered pattern from page 86.

Pick a point on the graph to begin your pencil line. Work slowly and move from square to square until the desired shape is completed. See illustration in the next column.

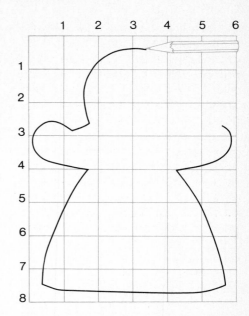

Transfer pattern from square to square.

GATHERING

Gathers are small, soft folds used to ease fabric and control fullness. Gathering can be done by hand or machine. The best fabrics to gather are fine and lightweight. Gathers should fall along the lengthwise threads of fabric, so stitches are made along the crosswise grain. Allow two to three times the finished width when determining the amount needed before gathering.

Divide the area to be gathered into sections. Leave gathering thread in place until final stitching is complete.

Hand Gathering—Use a double strand of strong thread. Sew a row of even running-stitches, on the right-side along the line to be gathered. Sew another row of stitches 1/4 inch away. Don't knot thread. Pull thread and ease fabric into gathers.

Machine Gathering—This produces an even effect. Gathers are easy to distribute. Loosen the upper tension on your sewing machine. Set the stitch gage at six stitches per inch. Sew a row of stitches on the right-side, along the line to be gathered. Make another row of stitches 1/4 inch above it in the seam allowance.

Ease the bobbin thread through

the fabric. Evenly distribute fullness from both ends. Wind each end of the drawn thread around a pin placed at right angles to the stitching. Work gathers until they are even, then fasten thread ends. Make several back-stitches to secure gathers.

To keep thread from breaking, divide the areas to be gathered into sections. Make separate rows of stitches for each section. For more on gathering, see *Ruffles*, page 17 and the *Party Dress*, page 74.

GLUING

Some projects involve gluing. Begin by putting down a cover to protect your work area. Use newspaper, a plastic dropcloth or some other spread. Newspaper is usually the most accessible, but newsprint may stain your project. A dropcloth or sheet is better when using spray adhesive.

Adhesive is a term for a group of compounds used to adhere materials to each other. Adhesives used in these projects include white glue, wood glue, spray adhesive, rubber cement and plastic glue. The materials list for each project indicates which is needed.

Tools—You need tools to help spread glue in an even, smooth manner. Some tools include a wood chopstick, ice-cream stick and toothpicks for applying glue to small areas. Tweezers and clamps are also useful. Tweezers are good for handling and placing small pieces to be glued, such as elements of the *News-Clipping Collage*, page 134. Clips or clothespins are useful for setting glued areas without slippage. See the *Covered Frames*, page 150.

White Glue—This is the best all-purpose glue. It sticks well to paper and cloth, and can be used successfully on wood and plastic. When applying white glue to cloth or paper, use it sparingly to prevent seepage that might be noticeable on the right-side of the project. White glue is waterproof.

Once it dries, it can't be removed. The tip of a toothpick is good for adding small amounts of white glue to a project.

Some projects, such as the *Covered Shape Box*, page 108, require a thin layer of white glue over the entire surface. Carefully spread the glue evenly with a wood ice-cream stick or other tool. If applying glue from the bottle, don't allow glue to settle in clumps before spreading.

Wood Glue—Wood glue is stronger than white glue. It is necessary for projects like wood toys that might receive rough wear. Do not use wood glue on paper or cloth.

Rubber Cement—This is stronger glue, but more expensive than white glue. There is less mess with rubber cement. Excess rubber cement can easily be rubbed away. It's good for spots of glue you want to dry hard and quickly.

Spray Adhesive—This type of glue is impractical for small detail gluing, but excellent for projects requiring gluing of entire surfaces. *Covered Albums*, page 153, and *Covered Frames*, page 150, use spray adhesive. Spray the adhesive lightly and evenly, following manufacturer's directions on the label.

Plastic Glue—Plastic glue is a strong adhesive designed for gluing plastic. It is necessary for projects, such as the *Recycled Clown* mobile, page 122, that would not hold together with any other kind of glue.

HANGING PICTURES

To hang pictures with wire, insert two screw eyes with shanks 1/8 inch to 1/4 inch long, depending on the size of your frame. A screw that is too large will split the frame. Insert the screw eyes 1/3 of the way down from the top of each side. They must be exactly even. Attach wire through the loops, allowing some slack. Leave enough of a tail on each side to twist the wire around itself.

HEMS AND HEM-STITCHES

A turned-up, finishing hem is used in many projects. Mark a hemline on the project. Match seam lines when pressing the hem in place. Adjust fullness between the seams. Trim bulk at seams by tapering edges 1/8 inch from hemline to the fold.

Pin or baste 1/2 inch above the edge and press the edge. If using pins, don't iron over them. Be sure pressed edges are even. Turn under the top raw edge or finish with bias tape. Press and stitch.

Hem-Stitch—This stitch is used for garment hems to hold the folded edge in place. Hold the garment toward you, and move the needle from right to left. The hem is held over the fingers of the left hand. Pick up a thread from the fabric below the folded edge of the hem. Next, pick up a thread from the folded edge of the hem. Repeat until hem is complete. See illustration below.

Hem-stitch

Invisible-Stitch—This is also called the *blind-hem stitch*. It is a way to sew hems and facings in place. Stitches are almost invisible on the right-side and wrong-side.

Finish the raw edge of the hem or facing. Roll it back about 1/4 inch, and attach thread securely. Sew a small stitch under one thread of the garment. Pick up one thread of the facing or hem a little farther along. Leave stitches fairly loose. This stitch may also be used on some sewing machines. See illustration below.

Invisible-stitch

Slip-Stitch—This is the best method to use when matching stripe or check fabrics and for lapping curved seams. Seams are tacked together from the right-side so they are in place before permanent stitching. The edge of a hem can be held down invisibly by slip-stitching.

This stitch is used for sewing a hem when stitching needs to be invisible on both sides. Start with the right-side of the fabric on top. Turn under one seam allowance. Position it over the other, which is kept flat.

Place pins at right angles to the seam. Pick up a single thread of fabric below the fold. Bring the needle through to the right-side at the fold, 1/2 inch to the left. Insert the needle below the fold underlayer, and make a stitch of the same length. Continue alternating stitches in the below-fold. See illustration below.

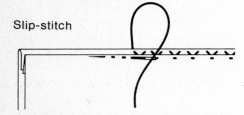
Slip-stitch

Whip-Stitch—This is a type of overcasting in which tiny stitches are used. For a description of the method, see *Overcasting*, page 11.

INTERFACING

In baby and toddler clothes, interfacing is sometimes used to give body to fabric. In the *Sunbonnet*, page 78, interfacing is used to give body to the brim. Interfacing is applied to fabric in other kinds of craft projects, such as the *Covered Frames*, page 150, and *Covered Albums*, page 153.

Interfacing can be woven or nonwoven, fusible or non-fusible. Fusible interfacing may be required in projects in this book. On one side of the fabric there is a heat-sensitive adhesive. Refer to package instructions for directions on application. In some projects, such as the *Sunbonnet*, page 78, non-fusible interfacing is required. It is heavier and gives the fabric more body.

When buying interfacing, there are many weights and fibers to choose from. Interfacing should be compatible with your fabric. It should give the fabric body and have the same care requirements.

MITERING

Mitering seam binding helps eliminate bulk at corners. It involves folds, either at right angles or 45° angles to the seam or strip. The procedure is similar for other types of corners. See the *Padded Sheets*, page 50.

Binding Outside Corners—With right-sides together, pin and stitch binding along the edges up to the seam allowance at the corner. This leaves the seam allowance free of binding. Secure stitches with a back-stitch, page 9. See illustration below.

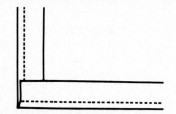
Seam allowance free of binding

Fold the strip diagonally at the corner. Pin, tack and stitch along the outer seam line to the edge of the garment or quilt. Turn binding to the inside. This forms a miter at the corner on the right-side. On the wrong-side, make a second folded miter in the other direction. This avoids excess bulk. See illustration below. Miter folds in place.

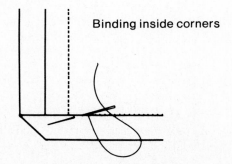
Binding inside corners

Binding Inside Corners—Stay-stitch the garment, and clip along the edges. Pull out the clipped edges. Pin and tack binding to the right-side, then stitch from the wrong-side of the garment. Make a miter in the right-side. Pull the fold to the wrong-side through the clipped edges. Turn the binding over the seam. Make a miter in the opposite direction.

Pin and tack the binding in place. Slip-stitch the miter folds and the binding. Remove tacking and press. See illustration below.

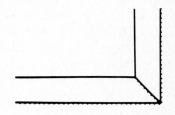
Finished mitered corner

PATCH POCKETS

Most pockets on the projects in this book are simple, unlined patch pockets. They are often made from self-fabric, such as those on the *Snappy Turtle*, page 104.

To make an unlined, square patch pocket, measure fabric in the desired size. Add 1/4 inch to the seam allowances at the sides and bottom. Add 1 inch at the top as facing. Cut out the pockets.

Reinforce the top edge with interfacing on the wrong-side. Turn under the seam allowance, press and stitch. Fold the 1/4-inch facing allowance to the right-side and press. Edge-stitch the facing along the seam allowances.

Miter bottom corners by trimming them diagonally 1/8 inch beyond stitching. Tack seam allowances to lessen bulk. Fold a corner of the fabric so it touches the intersection of the two merging tackings. Tack along the fold and press. To finish the back of the pocket, hand-baste around the edges and slip-stitch the facing to the pocket.

To make a pocket with rounded corners, cut a cardboard template the exact shape of the finished pocket. Sew a row of gathering stitches around the cut-out pocket edge. Ease-stitch along the seam line on the curve on each side. For information on *Easing*, see page 9. Turn pocket edges over to the wrong-side, and pull easing threads to adjust the fit. Press, then remove the cardboard, and tack edges in place.

To attach pockets, mark the pocket placement on the right-side of the project. Match lines, then pin and baste the finished patch pocket to the right-side of the project. Stitch the sides and bottom by machine or hand. If sewing by hand, use a slip-stitch. To avoid puckering the pocket, don't pull thread tight.

PATTERNS

Some patterns in this book are shown in reduced size and need to be enlarged. See page 12 for information on *Enlarging Patterns*. Other patterns are simple shapes, such as circles, squares or rectangles. See the *Diaper Backpack*, page 44.

Try to be accurate when making any pattern. For squares and rectangles, use a yardstick, T-square or other device. To make a perfect circle, use a compass or trace around a plate, saucer or bowl.

Making Patterns—Use a pencil or fabric marker to draw patterns. Don't use felt-tip pens that bleed. Ink passes through the absorbent tissue onto your fabric.

You may need to make a template that will be used many times, such as the 4-1/2-inch square needed for the *Gift Stocking*, page 155. Make multiple copies of the template. This keeps the pattern from wearing out, thus becoming inaccurate. Another technique is to trace the pattern on a sturdier surface such as cardboard. This makes fewer copies necessary.

Cutting Patterns—To cut patterns from plastic or cardboard, use a sharp knife or single-edge blade. For patterns that must be enlarged, seam lines are shown on the pattern, along with seam allowances. For patterns you measure yourself, trace the patterns on the wrong-side of the fabric. The lines you trace are the seam lines. Add 1/4 inch for seam allowances.

When making patchwork quilts, the same shape may be repeated many times, such as the square blocks in the *Appliquéd Patchwork Quilts*, page 26, or the diagonals in the wild-goose chase of *Andrew's Primary Quilt*, page 30. Instead of tracing the same template dozens of times, work and sew the fabric so multiples are made at the same time. For this simple process, see *Piecing Square and Diagonal Blocks*, page 16.

PIECING

Piecing is sewing together blocks or strips of fabric in a certain order to form a large, pieced length of fabric. Accuracy is the key to successful piecing.

To make pieces lie flat and fit together, they must be a uniform size and cut on the same grain. Fabric must also be prepared before piecing. To prevent possible shrinkage or bleeding when piecing is finished, prewash fabric. For examples of piecework, refer to the section on *Keepsake Quilts*, beginning on page 22.

Piecing Square Blocks—To make sets of light and dark blocks, begin with the lighter fabric. Marks show up well on light fabric. Place fabric face down on the table. Mark the fabric with a colored pencil or other non-permanent marker. See page 20 for information on *Fabric Markers*.

When lines are drawn, pin light and dark fabric with right-sides together. Match edges exactly. Stitch fabric together on the sewing machine with a straight-stitch. When you reach the end of

one row, don't cut the thread. Loosen it and turn the fabric so stitches don't pucker. See illustration below.

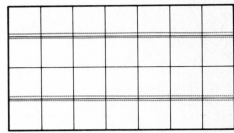
Stitch fabric together with a straight stitch.

When sewing is finished, remove pins and place the fabric piece on the table. Cut along the ruled lines. Open each set of stitched blocks and iron seams toward the darker fabric.

To sew light and dark blocks in strips, match two sets of fabric with right-sides together. Match raw edges so blocks of the same colors alternate and do not face each other. Pin each set so pins are out of the way of the sewing-machine needle.

Do not cut the thread between sets. Without allowing slack, stitch the two sets of blocks together along one short side. See illustration below. When you are finished, cut threads and iron seams to the darker side. The strips of four alternating light and dark squares can be sewn in a longer row.

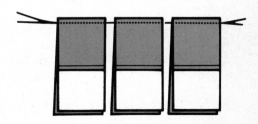
Stitch two sets of blocks together.

To vary this design in blocks, such as those used in the *Applique Patchwork Quilts*, page 26, stitch blocks along the long end rather than the short side. See illustration on page 16.

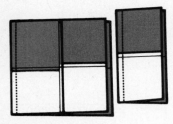

Stitch blocks along long edge.

Piecing Diagonal Blocks—For designs including diagonal squares, see the wild-goose chase and streak o' lightning patterns in *Andrew's Primary Quilt,* page 33.

To piece diagonal blocks, mark the lighter fabric on the back as indicated by solid lines. See illustration below. With raw edges

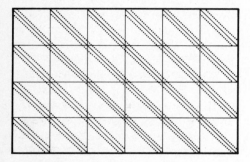

Mark fabric on back.

together, match the light and dark fabrics, with right-sides together. Sew 1/4-inch seams as indicated. When you reach the end of one row, do not cut the thread. Cut along the bold lines. Open the squares and iron both seams to the darker fabric. Clip protruding fabric on the two corners. See illustration below.

Iron both seams toward darker side.

PLASTIC

Different types of pliable plastic material are sold in fabric, hardware and craft stores. Plastic is sold by the foot and comes in different weights. You usually find light, medium and heavy plastic. These sheets often come with sug-

gested uses. Most of the projects in this book work with a lightweight, clear plastic. It is easier to sew and provides the protection you want.

Flimsier, less-expensive plastic is sold as a dropcloth. It is often cloudy or tinted, but can be used to cover the foam inserts of the *Bumper Pads,* page 36. A dropcloth is ideal for covering your work area.

PLEATS

Pleats are decorative folds in fabric. They control fullness and give extra width to a garment or project.

To make pleats, spread fabric on a flat surface where pleats can lie flat. Mark all folds clearly. Pleat folds are lapped to make the pleat. Tack fold and lap lines in different-color thread to avoid confusion.

Turn fabric to the right-side and lap folds to the broken line. Keep upper edges even. Pin and tack folds, then press gently. Stitch pleats from the bottom up. Stitching down may cause material to stretch and become distorted.

Inverted Pleat—These are box pleats in reverse. Two pleats are turned toward each other. The inverted pleat is used in the *Welcome-Baby Wreath,* page 140.

Mark the fold line, center line and placement line with pins or tailor's chalk. Create the fold lines of the pleat. Press down to the placement line.

Pin pleats at the placement line, and tack in position. Stitch through all layers of fabric. Press and remove tacking. Press again for a crisp finish.

PREPARING TO SEW

Before laying out your pattern, prepare your fabric. Preparing fabric will straighten the grain, remove sizing and make your project easier to work with.

On woven fabrics, the first step is to check the grain. Weaving is one of the most common ways of

making yarn into fabric. Two sets of thread run at right angles to each other in woven fabric. *Warp* is the lengthwise set of threads that run parallel to the selvage. These threads are strong. In a simple weave, the crosswise, or *weft,* threads run over and under warp threads. These are also called *straight grains.*

If both weft and warp are slanted, the fabric is *off grain.* Cut pieces from fabric with the two grains at right angles to one another. Pieces cut *on the grain* maintain their shape and hang well. Those cut *off grain* may be a failure. The true bias is a line at a 45° angle from the straight grain.

Sometimes after storage or handling, the warp and weft do not run at right angles to each other. Look at the cut length of fabric to see if it is crooked or if the grain is not straight.

If it is not obvious which is the right-side of the fabric, look at the selvage. A selvage is the finished edge that runs along both sides of the fabric. Selvages are usually rougher and more uneven on the *wrong-side* of the fabric.

Before you cut or sew, straighten fabric ends and straighten the grain. Preshrink fabric and find the right-side.

Straightening Fabric Ends—Before working with fabric, check the grain and straighten it, if necessary. To do this, you need a straight edge along the crosswise grain. This straight edge can be made by tearing, drawing a thread or cutting along a prominent line.

Tearing—Only tightly woven fabric can be torn along the crosswise grain. If fabric will tear, snip the selvage. Grasp the fabric on either side of the snip and rip across to the other selvage. For more information on tearing, see the section on *Borders and Backgrounds* for *Appliqué Patchwork Quilts,* page 27.

Drawing Thread—If your fabric is loosely woven or stretchy, snip in the selvage at one end. Pull a crosswise thread until the fabric puckers. Cut along this puckered line to the selvage at the other side.

Cut Along Prominent Lines— This method involves cutting along a crosswise line of fabric with a linear design, such as plaid, check and stripe. Lay your fabric flat on a surface, then cut the entire length along one design line.

Straightening Grain—When you locate the crosswise thread, check to see if the fabric is on grain. Occasionally, grains are no longer at right angles to each other. Make grains even before you begin your project.

Fold the fabric lengthwise, and match selvages and ends. The abric is off grain if the edges do not align along all three edges. Straighten the fabric before you begin.

If fabric is only slightly off grain, straighten the crosswise grain of the second end. Fold the fabric lengthwise, with right-sides together. Pin every few inches along the selvages and ends. Press from the selvage to the fold, working the weave in the correct direction.

If fabric is off grain, it must be stretched. For washable fabric, dampen or wash it to make threads more pliable. Fabric is stretched by pulling it along the bias. Pull firmly but gently so fabric forms right angles at all corners. Don't stretch too far or the grain line will be more distorted.

Preparing Knit Fabric—With knits or stretch fabrics, there are no selvages. Threads can't be pulled. Some flat knits have perforated lengthwise edges comparable to a woven selvage. These edges are usually not straight and can't be used for alignment.

Knit fabric comes in tubular and flat forms. For straightening the ends of a flat knit, baste the entire length of two opposite sides. Fold fabric lengthwise, align markings and pin together.

To straighten the ends of a tubular knit, cut it open along one rib.

Prewashing—Use washable fabric for all projects a baby wears or plays with. Prewash fabric to remove excess chemicals and resins. This also ensures fabric doesn't shrink when the project is finished. When buying fabric, check laundering instructions on the fabric bolt, then wash and dry the fabric. When dry, press the fabric to remove creases and wrinkles.

Finding Right-Side of Fabric— The right-side of the fabric may be obvious. Sometimes you must take a closer look. On the right-side of woven fabric, the selvage is smoother, printed designs are sharper and texture is softer, shinier or slicker. On the right-side of textured fabrics, the texture is more distinct. On the wrong-side you often find irregularities, such as extra-thick nubs.

REINFORCING STITCHES

Reinforcing stitches may be necessary for points of strain. Points of strain include the bottom of openings, buttonholes or the tops of pockets. There are different ways to add this extra strength. You can add a small piece of seam binding under the top of each pocket. The simplest way is to sew a double row of stitches. Stitch about 1 inch on either side of the point, inside the seam line. You can also tack points of stress.

RUFFLES

A ruffle can be an excellent finish for many baby items. It is easily made for a small cost. Premade ruffling may also be purchased. See the *Changing Pad,* page 35.

A straight ruffle is made from a continuous strip of fabric or several strips sewn together. Cut ruffling strips on the bias. Bias-cut ruffles create softer folds. Cut fabric two to three times the length of the edge to which it is applied. Cut wide ruffles longer to make them look full.

For a single ruffle, cut a strip of fabric the desired width, plus a hem and seam allowance. On one edge, fold the raw edges under 1/4 inch and press. Fold under 1/4 inch again, press and machine- or hand-stitch. For a double ruffle, cut a strip of fabric twice the desired width, plus two seam allowances. Fold the strip lengthwise, with wrong-sides together. Sew the raw edge of the ruffle to the raw edge of the garment or project.

Ruffling can be done by hand or machine. To make a ruffle, sew two rows of basting-stitches on the ruffling fabric. Sew one row along the seam line and the other 1/4 inch above it, in the seam allowance.

To form the ruffle, draw up the basting threads. See illustration below. When working with a short strip, secure both threads at one end. Gather from the opposite end. For longer strips, gather one end, sew the threads, then gather at the opposite end. For extra-long ruffles, gather in quarters.

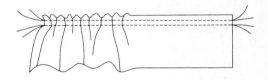

Making ruffle

Adding Ruffles—A ruffle may be added to a straight seam or a faced edge. Pin the ruffle to the right-side of project. Match raw edges with the finished side of the ruffle facing the inside. See the illustration for the *Tied Quilt,* page 23. Evenly distribute gathers. If ruffling is long, divide it in sections before pinning it to the edge.

You may want to attach a long ruffle to an area that is not straight. This is done in the *Party Dress,* page 74. Skirt tiers are attached to one another and to the bodice. Before pinning, divide the ruffle into sections, and mark it with pins. Divide the side the ruffle is attached to into the same number of sections. Mark the fabric with pins, match them and pin together.

Pull the gathering threads to evenly adjust ·fullness. Pin between markings with the ruffle-side up, and stitch along the seam line. Pin the other side of the seam over the ruffled edge, with right-sides together. Stitch inside the first row of stitching. Press the seam allowance away from the ruffle and turn to the right-side.

SEAM ALLOWANCES

When sewing is finished, trim seam allowances in places where extra fabric adds bulk, such as sleeve and crotch seams. Also trim seams that will be enclosed, such as facings, collars and cuffs.

Most seam allowances are trimmed to 1/4 inch. *Grading* is cutting one side of the seam shorter than the other. This is needed for thick fabrics and for more than two layers of fabric. For turning this graded allowance into a finished seam, see the *Kimono Jacket*, page 69.

Clipping—With seam allowances trimmed to 1/4 inch, clip inside and outside curves. This reduces tension on the seams, and seams will lie flat. Clip into seam allowances 1/16 inch from the seam. Be careful not to clip stitching. More clipping is needed for sharper curves than for gradual ones.

SEARING

This is a method of scorching or melting the surface of synthetic fabric. In the *Diaper Backpack*, page 44, the ends of the nylon web are seared to prevent fraying. Hold a match over the area to be seared, and nylon will begin to melt. Extinguish the match to prevent further melting.

STRIPS FOR TIES, LOOPS, STRAPS AND SASHES

Making Strips—Cut a strip of fabric twice the desired width measurement, plus 1/2 inch for a 1/4-inch seam allowance. Fold the fabric in half widthwise, matching raw edges. Press.

Begin at the fold of the short end. Stitch across this end to within 1/4 inch of the corner. Turn the fabric and stitch the entire length. Leave the last short side open. Turn the strip right-side out, and fold raw edges inward. Press, then sew the opening closed.

Variations—When strips are narrow or when many are required for braiding, such as for the *Braided Rocker Cover*, page 52, there is an easier method. Strips are top-stitched and do not need to be turned right-side out. To make these strips, fold and iron the raw edges of each short end to the wrong-side. Do the same for each long edge, so all raw edges are turned to the inside.

Fold the strip in half along its length, matching the edges. Iron and pin or baste edges together. Top-stitch the entire length by hand or machine.

When making a sash, such as for the *Robe*, page 70, add body to the strip with fusible interfacing before stitching. Cut interfacing the same length, but only half the width of the strip. If you prefer, instead of cutting the corners square, taper them to a gradual point on each side.

STUFFING

Many of the projects in this book require stuffing. Projects are stuffed with different materials, such as polyester fiber, mattress pads, foam rubber and hosiery.

Polyester Fiber—*Polyfill* is the most frequently used polyester fiber. It is clean to work with and washable. Polyfill comes in one pound bags or rolled sheets. The sheets come in different weights, such as 3 ounce, 6 ounce, 12 ounce or 24 ounce. The 3-ounce size is ideal for covering picture frames and albums.

Any weight may be used for stuffing a quilt. The weight you choose depends on how thick you want your quilt to be. Lighter weights are better for hand- or machine-quilting. Weights that are heavier are better for tying.

Mattress Pads—A good way to recycle mattress pads is to use them as batting. They must be evenly worn. Mattress pads are easy to machine-quilt. Used mattress pads make an ideal middle layer for the *Denim Infant-Seat Cover*, page 40, and the *Padded Sheets*, page 50.

Mattress pads that are new or in good shape can be used for other projects. The mattress pad is the quilted fabric needed for the project. For this type of use, see the *Reversible Play Mat*, page 35, the *Fitted Infant-Seat Cover*, page 40, and the *Car-Seat Cover*, page 38.

Foam Rubber—Foam rubber comes in bags and sheets. Bags are filled with shredded foam, which is messy to work with, but ideal for some projects. Polyfill that isn't tied or quilted loses shape in water, so foam rubber is used in the bathtub *Clutch Toys*, page 88.

The *Bumper Pads*, page 36, are stuffed with foam blocks cut from sheets. This kind of stuffing prevents the problem of washing large fiber-filled sections. Six fiber-stuffed cushions are a laundry load. Because sections are large and usually not quilted or tied, batting looses form when washed and has to be replaced. Foam inserts for the pads are easily removed before each washing. The fabric cover for each pad takes up no more room in the washing machine than a top sheet for a single bed.

Hosiery—In the past, shredded hosiery and other rags were often used for stuffing. These materials can still be used, especially for dolls and toys. The only projects in this book that use hosiery are the *Yarn Dolls*, page 95. Part of the project requires the feet from a pair of pantyhose or stockings.

You can use old hose when you make this project. Shredded nylon stuffed inside the toe lends itself to sculpturing the doll's face. Pack as many shreds as possible into the doll's head, working them in place from the wrong-side.

Stuffing Methods—When stitching something to be stuffed, leave a 1- to 2-inch opening, depending on the size of the object to be stuffed. Make this opening at an easy-access area, such as the body of a doll rather than a hand or foot area.

If using polyfill, fluff each handful before inserting it in the opening. Pull each handful apart and put it back together several times. This process helps avoid uneven knotting or bunching of fibers when the object is stuffed.

Begin by stuffing the smallest areas farthest from the opening. To reach fingers, toes, ends of beaks and other hard-to-reach places, use a stuffing tool to push fiber in place. This tool can be a chopstick, crochet hook or other long device that won't tear fabric. Wrap a small amount of batting around the end of the tool, then gently push the polyfill in place.

Fill in surrounding areas farthest from the opening, such as arms and legs. Continue stuffing a little batting at a time. Pack it firmly as you work your way toward the opening.

If you add a musical device, such as a bell, wrap it with batting before inserting it in the toy. Then baby won't be hurt by the object being too close to the surface.

When you finish stuffing, let the doll or toy sit overnight before stitching the opening closed. As fiber settles, you may find the stuffing is not as firmly packed as you wanted.

Sew the opening closed with a slip-stitch, page 14. If stuffing an appliqué, you may want to use a buttonhole-stitch or other decorative stitch. For information on cutting, sewing and stuffing appliqués, see *Appliqués* page 6.

TUCKS

A tuck is a stitched fold of fabric and is often used for decorative purposes. In these projects, it is used as a shaping device.

Make tucks before laying out pattern pieces. It's easier to tuck a large piece of fabric, then cut out the pattern piece from the already-tucked fabric. Tucks are evenly spaced or in groups of three or more.

Mark and sew one tuck before marking the next tuck. Pin and tack each tuck in place along its length. Keep the grain straight so one thread runs along the edge of each tuck.

Tack, then machine-stitch the tuck in place. Remove tacking and press each tuck lightly along the stitching line. When tucks are complete, lay out pattern pieces in the usual manner. Pin and cut out the pieces.

The width of tucking lines will vary. For baby clothes, lines will be narrow, called *pin tucks*. Wider tucks are called *spaced tucks* and *blind tucks*. If you make a tuck on the inside of fabric, mark lines on the wrong-side in the same manner as described above.

TYING

Quilt layers may be fastened together with ties rather than stitches. In this book, ties are made with yarn in the *Tied Quilt*, page 23, and the *Denim Infant-Seat Cover*, page 40. In the *Gift Stocking*, page 155, they are made with thread. Ties can also be made from crochet string, perle cotton or buttonhole twist.

To tie a quilt, thread a large needle with the chosen material. Take a stitch through the three layers from the top. Bring the needle back up a short distance away. Take a second stitch in the same place, then tie a square knot. See illustrations below. Cut the ends about 1 inch from the surface of the quilt.

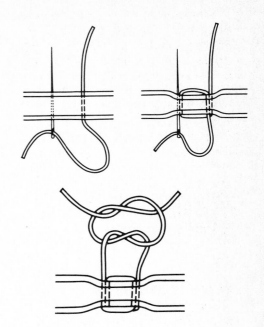

Tying quilt

EQUIPMENT

You will need different equipment for different projects. This section discusses what you will need. As you develop sewing skills and work on other projects, you may need other supplies. For lists of other supplies, check sewing books listed in the *Bibliography*, page 158.

Basic tools for sewing include cutting tools, marking tools, ironing equipment, measuring tools, pins, needles and assorted threads.

CUTTING TOOLS

There are several kinds of scissors and cutting tools to use. Sewing projects in this book utilize four of these tools—embroidery scissors, dressmaker shears, pinking shears and a seam ripper. Before using scissors, test them first on scrap fabric.

Embroidery Scissors—These are useful for embroidery, as well as trimming, clipping and detail work. They are 5 to 6 inches long, have straight blades and the same-size rings for handles.

Dressmaker Shears—These are excellent for cutting fabric. The handle is bent or straight. A bent-angle handle lets fabric rest on the table or cutting surface while you cut. These shears are made in 6- to 12-inch lengths. The 7- to 8-inch size is used most frequently and is easiest to manage. Left-handed versions are also available.

Pinking Shears—These shears make a zigzag cut for finishing seams and raw edges of fabric. See the *Fabric Butterflies,* page 116. The zigzag cut keeps fabric from raveling. These scissors are not intended for cutting out pattern pieces. Blades come in lengths from 5-1/2 to 10-1/2 inches. The 7-1/2- to 9-inch blade is the most manageable. Pinking shears need to be oiled regularly and sharpened professionally.

Seam Ripper—This is a penlike object with a blade shaped like a hook on one end. It is used for removing machine- and hand-stitches. Be careful not to tear fabric when using it.

FABRIC-MARKING TOOLS

There are several ways to mark fabric. Avoid felt-tip pens or ink not specifically made for fabric. Don't use markers that bleed through fabric.

Dressmaker's Marking Pencils or Pens—These are available in fabric stores. Pencils usually have tailor's chalk at one end and a brush on the other. Pens are filled with water-soluble ink.

Tailor's Chalk—Colored squares are made from chalk or wax. With the help of a steam iron, wax may be easier to remove from hard-surfaced fabrics.

Dressmaker's Tracing Paper and Wheel—Kits are available, including a wide assortment of colors and double-faced and single-faced paper.

Needle and Thread—This is used to mark fabric with running-stitches, page 11.

Markers for Decorating the Out-side of Fabric—When making a project like the octopus in the *Stuffed Toys,* page 84, or *Cloth Books,* page 102, artwork is done directly on fabric. Visit an art or craft store and buy markers specifically for use on fabric. A felt-tip pen with permanent ink is not intended for use on fabric. It may bleed as the picture is being drawn. You can also use fabric crayons.

IRONING EQUIPMENT

One of the most important steps in sewing is ironing and pressing. Set up the ironing board as close to your sewing machine as possible. Press the project at each stage for a professional finish. There is a difference between pressing and ironing. *Pressing* is the process of lifting the iron up and setting it down in its proper position. *Ironing* is moving the iron over the fabric in a repeated, sliding movement.

For projects in this book, you need the equipment listed below.

Steam Iron—This can be used as a steam iron or used dry. It should have a wide range of temperatures, a spray device and many steam vents. Keep the bottom of the iron clean.

Ironing Board—Your ironing board should have a clean, padded cover.

Pressing Cloth—This is a piece of cheesecloth or fabric used between the iron and fabric to protect the fabric. A pressing cloth should be similar in weight to the weight of the fabric being pressed. An extra scrap of fabric that is used for the project is often a good pressing cloth.

Sleeve Board—This is an optional piece of equipment for your convenience. The sleeve board consists of two small, padded ironing boards connected to each other. They are used for ironing parts of a sewing project too small to fit around an ironing board, such as the sleeve of the *Party Dress,* page 74.

KNOTTING BOARD

A working surface may be needed for macramé, detailed knots or when you are learning to tie knots. The purpose of the board is to hold the material you are going to knot in place as you work. Boards can be made from many materials. You can use padded cardboard, cork, Styrofoam or any lightweight, rigid material in which you can stick pins. The board can be cut in any size to suit your needs. Some good sizes are 12x24" and 20x36".

MEASURING EQUIPMENT

Accurate measurements are essential for a successful project. Correct tools are needed for obtaining these measurements. The following tools are used for projects in this book.

French Curve—This tool is used for making curved edges. It is used to curve the top-flap corners of the *Diaper Backpack,* page 44. The same precision can be accomplished by other means, such as by using a compass or by tracing the curved edges of plates and saucers.

Ruler—A 12-inch, transparent ruler is useful for checking the grain line of fabric and marking buttonholes, tucks and single bias strips.

Tape Measure—This is the most important measuring tool for taking body measurements. Select a fiberglass or plastic tape that won't stretch or tear. The tape should have measurements on both sides.

T-square—T-squares are useful for locating cross grains, squaring edges and marking continuous bias. A transparent one, at least 9 inches long with a 4-inch span, is a good selection. A ruler or yardstick can also be used.

Yardstick—This tool is used for marking the bias, checking grain and taking long, straight measurements. Be sure the surface is smooth and clearly marked on both sides.

PINS AND NEEDLES

Before you can sew any projects, you need a good assortment of pins and needles. This section concentrates on pins for general sewing and needles for hand-sewing. Your sewing-machine handbook will give you information about sewing-machine needles.

Straight Pins—Straight pins are used to secure patterns to fabric or to hold fabric for stitching. Straight pins come with flat heads or round, colorful heads. Colored heads make pins easier to see.

Pins come in different lengths and thicknesses. Longer pins are usually thicker. The standard-length pin for most sewing projects is 1-1/16 inches. This pin is suitable for light- to medium-weight fabrics. Pins that are 1-1/4 inches long are good for heavier fabric. Other pin lengths are also available. Ball-point pins are fine pins with a round point that doesn't catch and snag fibers of knit fabrics.

T-Pins—These pins are wider pins with a T-shape head. They can also be used for heavy pile fabrics and loose knits. T-pins are used for attaching elements to the *Shower Wreath,* page 127, and the *Welcome-Baby Wreath,* page 140.

Hand-Sewing Needles—Needles come in different lengths and thicknesses, each designed for a particular use. Choose needles according to the fabric you will be sewing. Usually, each type of needle comes in a range of sizes and falls into one of two sizes—*1 to 10* and *14 to 22.* The larger the number, the shorter and finer the needle. The following list includes types of needles necessary for sewing and craft projects:

- Sharps—All-purpose needles, suitable for most fabrics, medium length, with round eyes.
- Betweens—Quilting needles, shorter than sharps with round eyes, good for making fine stitches through heavy fabric.
- Milliner's—Basting and gathering needles, long with round eyes.
- Embroidery—Medium-length needles with a long eye so several strands of embroidery floss can be threaded through it.
- Chenilles—Sharp, heavy embroidery needles to use with yarn when embroidering or tying quilts.

THREAD

A good thread is strong and durable. It has some elasticity and resists tangling. When choosing thread, choose one compatible with the fabric in color, weight and type. If colors can't be matched exactly, choose a thread slightly darker than the fabric. When sewing multicolored fabrics, choose a thread to match the dominant color.

Polyester Thread—This thread is available in different weights for specific purposes. All polyester thread, including cotton-wrapped polyester, provides strength and elasticity for sewing synthetic, knit and stretch fabrics.

Mercerized-Cotton Thread—This thread is 100% cotton, with no stretch or give. It is suitable for most general sewing, especially woven, natural-fiber fabrics. Size 50 is medium thickness and can be used for hand- or machine-sewing on light- and medium-weight fabrics. Lower-number threads are suitable for heavier fabrics. Other types of cotton thread include button-and-carpet thread and quilting thread for hand- or machine-sewing.

Silk Thread—Silk thread is a fine, lustrous thread, known for its durability and elasticity. It is ideal for use with silk and fine wool fabrics. For projects in this book, it might be used for embroidery work or mobiles. The size is given in letters. Size A is suitable for general sewing and basting. Size D is suitable for gathering, thread loops, hand-worked buttonholes and attaching buttons.

Nylon Thread—Nylon thread is strong and made from one continuous filament. It is used for heavy-duty work on fabric and is suitable for hanging some light mobiles. Nylon thread is clear or available in colors. It is the least heat-resistant of all threads. Do not use it on fabrics requiring a high heat setting on the iron.

OTHER SEWING AIDS

There are other sewing aids and notions you may need to complete a project. Check this list before you begin.

Hoops—For embroidery and appliqué, you may need an embroidery hoop. This consists of two rings of metal, wood or plastic that fit together to hold fabric taut. These hoops come in many sizes. Embroidery hoops may also be used as inexpensive frames for fabric. See the *T-Shirt Mobile,* page 124, and *Children's Embroidery-Hoop Projects,* page 115.

Large hoops are made for quilting. You can usually find them in fabric and craft stores. Before buying a quilting hoop, check the size and style you need. Some hoops can be made at home. See the quilting references in the *Bibliography,* page 158.

Beeswax—Beeswax is convenient for hand-sewing. It is a resinous substance that comes in solid blocks encased in plastic. Slots in the plastic allow thread to be passed through the beeswax. This makes it stronger and more resistant to tangles. You can also use thread that had a glace or smooth finish for hand-sewing.

Thimble—A thimble protects fingertips. You need to wear a thimble when you are sewing fabric that is heavy or thick.

Keepsake Quilts

A quilt can be practical and decorative. Whether quilted with puffs, ties, hand- or machine-stitches, the end product is durable and homemade. You can use the quilt because it's washable, and you can display it because it's beautiful.

A baby quilt can be as simple or complex as you want to make it. If you are a beginning craftsperson, a small baby blanket makes a great first quilting project. You can start with the simple *Tied Quilt,* page 23, which has no detailed piecing, appliqué or quilting procedures. Look through your fabric scraps and you'll probably find some wonderful pieces to use for the patchwork squares.

If you are an experienced quilter, a small baby quilt can be a fine display of your best work. It can also serve as incentive for designing your own patchwork pattern. See *Andrew's Primary Quilt,* page 30, for samples of piecing designs you might choose for your own.

Even if you use your quilt in the crib, consider adding a tube for mounting. Make the tube from the same fabric as the backing. This hanging device is helpful when baby is too big to use the quilt any longer.

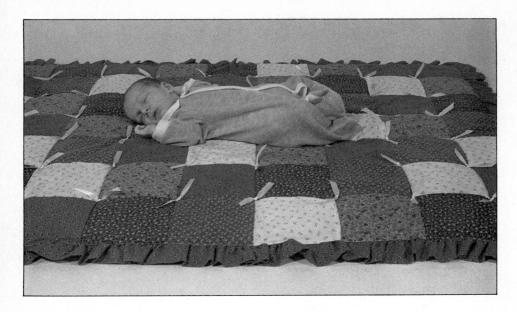

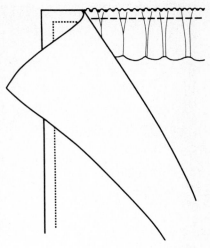

Figure A—When quilt is turned right-side out, ruffle is correctly positioned.

Tied Quilt

This quilt is quick and easy to make. The patchwork top can be sewn quickly, and the three layers are tied together with ribbon or yarn.

EQUIPMENT
- Pattern-making supplies, page 15
- Sewing supplies

MATERIALS
- 1 yard of 45-inch-wide fabric for backing
- 5 to 7 color-coordinated pieces, each 1/3 yard of 45-inch-wide fabric
- 1 yard 45-inch-wide batting, page 18
- 5-1/3 yards of yarn for ties
- 1 yard of 45-inch-wide fabric for ruffle
- 5-1/3 yards of ribbon for ties, optional

MAKING TOP
Make a 5-1/2-inch template, page 12, and transfer 63 squares to your fabric. See page 20 for information on marking fabric. Cut squares from fabric. After pieces are cut, arrange them in seven rows of nine pieces each. Stitch the squares in rows with 1/4-inch seams on all sides, then stitch rows together.

MAKING RUFFLE
Cut the fabric for the ruffle in six 6-inch strips. With right-sides facing, stitch the short ends together to form one long strip. Make the ruffle by hand or with a machine. See page 17.

JOINING SIDES
With right-sides facing, put the top and bottom pieces together. Place the ruffle around the edge inside the two pieces. See page 17 for information about adding ruffles and see Figure A. Pin and baste the layers, page 9, then stitch three sides together. Leave one short end open. Turn the quilt right-side out and stuff. Do not close the last side until tying is complete.

TYING
To stabilize the three layers, baste the quilt together. See page 6. If using yarn, thread a long strand of yarn through a sharp needle. See page 20 for information on needles. Don't tie a knot in the yarn or thread. Find the point where squares meet inside the seams. Stitch down through all three layers, leaving a few inches of yarn on top. See page 19 for information on tying quilts.

If using ribbon, cut it into 48 4-inch strips. After the thread is tied, use the long ends to tie a ribbon in place. Then tie the ribbon in a knot or bow before beginning the next tie.

FINAL SEWING
Sew the open short end after all tying is complete. You can sew the seam by hand or on your sewing machine.

Puff Quilt

This is one quilt baby doesn't have to outgrow. Individual pillows are stitched together, so you can add new rows of pillows anytime. Make pillows from scraps left from projects you have worked on. Whether made with small hexagons, squares or rectangles, the quilt can record projects made during a lifetime.

SIZE
The size of the quilt varies. The one shown here is made to fit a port-a-crib. It is 29x43'' or 293 pillows made in 15 alternating rows of 20 and 19. The hexagon pattern is used for this quilt. The pattern is shown on page 90.

EQUIPMENT
- **Pattern-making supplies, page 15**
- **Sewing supplies**

MATERIALS
- **Scraps of washable cotton and polyester fabric. Small shapes, such as hexagons, take longer to make, but they use less than 6x3-1/2'' for each pillow.**
- **Thread for sewing machine**

Or
- **Hand quilter's thread, page 21**
- **Polyfill, page 18**

MAKING PUFFS
See page 12 for making multiple copies of a pattern. It is easiest to make pillows in groups. Trace the pattern on the fabric as many times as possible. Leave room for a 1/4-inch seam allowance around the outline of each pillow. Do *not* cut the pattern pieces from the fabric.

Place two pieces of fabric with right-sides together. Match the marked fabric piece with an unmarked fabric piece the same size. Pin or baste, then machine- or hand-stitch each hexagon on five sides.

Cut the pillows 1/4 inch from the seam line. Turn each pillow right-side out and stuff. See Figure A. Close the gap with a slip-stitch. See page 14.

SEWING PUFFS TOGETHER
Sew the puffs in rows. Work two puffs at a time. See Figure B. Knot thread at the beginning and end. Use a slip-stitch to join the inside seams. See Figures C and D.

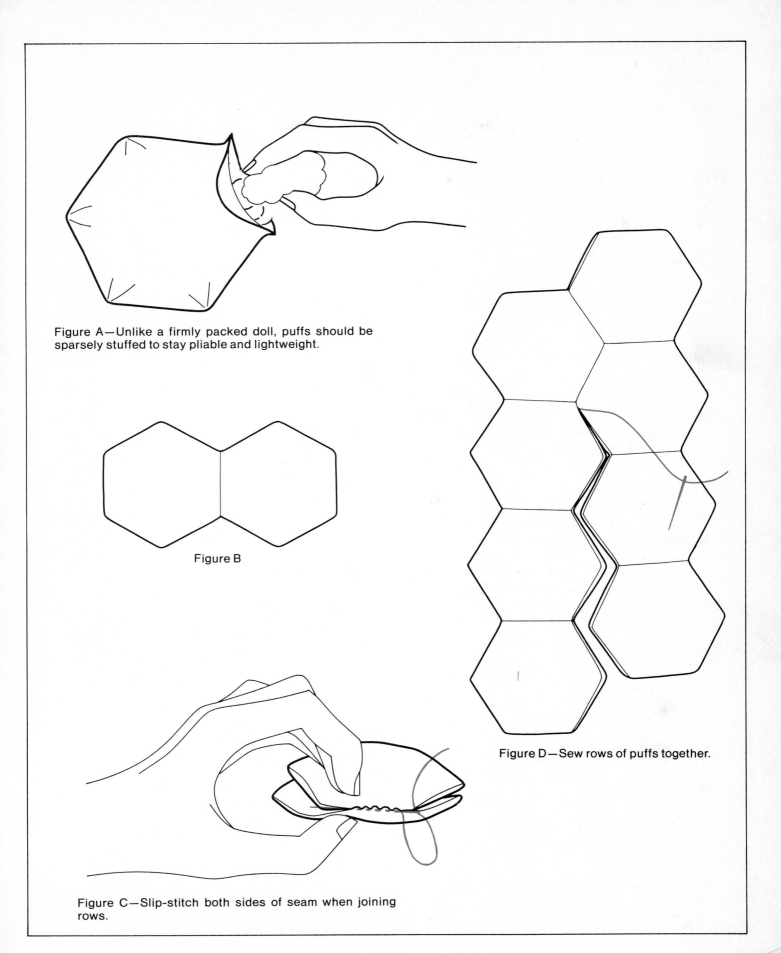

Figure A—Unlike a firmly packed doll, puffs should be sparsely stuffed to stay pliable and lightweight.

Figure B

Figure D—Sew rows of puffs together.

Figure C—Slip-stitch both sides of seam when joining rows.

Duck Quilt

Animal Quilt

Appliqué Patchwork Quilts

These quilts combine modern with traditional. Ready-made appliqués can be used to decorate machine-pieced tops. Quilting and embroidery are done by hand.

EQUIPMENT
- Pattern-making supplies, page 15
- Quilting needles. Short, hairpin needles, size 8 to 10, sometimes called betweens, see page 21.
- Ruler or yardstick, page 20
- No. 2 pencil for transferring pattern on pale-color fabric
- White pencil or charcoal for dark colors
- Water-solvent pen to mark quilting design. Test all water-solvent pens on scrap fabric before applying to quilt.
- Quilter's frame or large, round or oval embroidery hoop
- Thimble
- Water sprayer for removing water-solvent ink, optional

MATERIALS
The quilts shown in the photograph are 40x46" and 43x49". The size of your quilt depends on the size and number of appliqués you use. This is determined on graph paper. See the section on *Graphing* at right.

Make the front and back of your quilt from 100% cotton. There are two reasons for not using polyester. Polyester batting bleeds through polyester fabric in tiny beads. Also, polyester stretches as you work with it. This makes accuracy almost impossible to achieve. See page 16 for information on preparing fabric.

- 1-1/3 yard of 45-inch-wide fabric for backing
- 1 yard of 45-inch-wide fabric for bias, page 6
- 1 or more appliqués
- Polyester thread for machine-stitching
- Cotton quilting thread with a glace finish
- 1-1/3 yard of 45-inch-wide batting, page 18

GRAPHING A PATTERN
Plot your quilt design on graph paper. See Figure A. Use crayons or colored pencils to test colors. Make several arrangements of blocks and borders before deciding on one design. This eliminates guesswork when piecing the top. You'll know the exact placement of each block. It also helps prevent problems, such as uneven color distribution. You can determine the correct number of blocks and borders to cut, saving time and expense.

You must know the size of your appliqués. Measure the dimensions and reduce the measurement to fit the graph. The backing needs to be 1-1/2 to 2 inches bigger than the top on all sides until quilting is complete.

Frame the appliqués with blocks and borders. Blocks can be arranged with light and dark colors contrasting to form a checkerboard pattern. Borders are strips of fabric in a solid color. In the Duck Quilt, above, the checkerboard alternates with the border. In the Animal Quilt, above, each appliqué is framed twice by a checkerboard, except for single rows on the sides.

Figure A—Quilting pulls material. Top measuring 42x48" on graph paper might be 40x46" when finished.

With right-sides together, match the seams of the first border and the background of the appliqué. Pin and baste strips to the appliquéd square before machine-stitching. Attach the bottom row in the same way. When stitching is complete, iron the stitched seams toward the darker fabric. Next, sew the side strips. Follow the same order of pinning, stitching and ironing.

To overlap seam endings, alternate the order in which strips are sewn. If you begin with the top and bottom strips, then sew side strips. Next begin with the sides, followed by the top and bottom. Continue alternating until piecing is complete. See Figure B.

If working with more than one appliqué, sew a frame around each background piece. Stitch sections together, working from the center out.

Figure B—Accuracy is important when piecing. A mismatched line can impair design.

MAKING STRIPS OF BLOCKS FROM FABRIC

See page 15 for information on making patchwork blocks. Sew blocks in contrasting sets, then iron the stitched sets to the darker fabric. Pin sets together to form strips, keeping seams matched and alternating light and dark colors. Use a 1/4-inch seam to stitch the sets in single rows.

BORDERS AND BACKGROUNDS

For borders and backgrounds, add 1/2 inch to the measurement on the graph paper. When using 100% cotton, tear borders or long strips of fabric for more-even results. Mark the top and bottom edges along the straight grain of the fabric. Snip, then tear. Since tearing curls the edge of fabric, iron fabric after it is torn. If using a polyester blend, cut fabric strips and backgrounds for appliqués.

PIECING

Center your appliqué on the background piece. Baste in place and embroider the outline with the buttonhole-stitch, page 10. Appliqués with back pieces, such as the duck's, are added when quilting is complete.

MARKING DESIGN

Mark the pieced top for the quilting design before the top, bottom and batting are basted together. Lay the top on a clean table. Using a yardstick or ruler as a guide, mark the blocks around the appliquéd backgrounds with your water-solvent pen.

The diamond pattern makes diamond-shapes on the quilted back piece. It is used on both of these quilts. To make this pattern, draw diagonal lines from one corner to the opposite corner of each block. Complete all parallel lines, then draw lines that intersect. See Figure C. On the appliqué, quilt around certain details. On the Duck Quilt, page 26, the petals of the hat are quilted along with the eye, bill, neck piece and upper legs.

Figure C—Quilting design on blocks can be carried over to appliquéd background.

CUTTING BACKGROUND AND BASTING

The *exact* measurement for the backing will not be known until you make the top. To allow for differences, cut the backing 1-1/2 to 2 inches larger on all sides than the pieced top. This eliminates the problem of not allowing enough fabric. When quilting is complete, before adding bias, trim excess fabric. This technique is described in the section *Trimming Back Piece* on page 29.

To prepare for basting, lay your materials on the table in the following order:

1. Quilt backing, with the right-side facing the table.

2. Batting, centered on top of backing.

3. Quilt top, with right-side facing you.

Pin the layers around the edges. Baste the layers together to prevent slippage, page 6.

QUILTING

When your quilt is well-basted, stretch it taut and smooth on the quilting frame or hoop. Cut pieces of quilting thread about 16 inches long. If thread is longer, it breaks or you get knotting problems.

One way to avoid knotting problems and ensure maximum strength is to thread your needle from the spool. Knot your thread at the cut end. When pulling stitches taut, pull the *thread*, not the needle.

Begin by quilting details of the appliqué. Make a small knot, then push the needle and knot through the top fabric, into the batting. It should be a short distance from where you will be quilting. Bring the needle up through the marked line, and lightly tug the knot in place.

Work toward yourself or in a more-comfortable direction. Return the needle down through the top of your pattern. See Figure D.

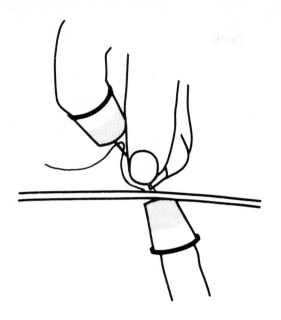

Figure D—By working from center out, make one stitch at a time.

Quilting can be done two ways, depending on your preference. The first is to make one stitch at a time and enter the fabric at an acute angle.

The second method is to quilt with a running-stitch, page 11. Do three or four stitches at a time. See Figure E. Make stitches even and as small as possible. The number of stitches to an inch depends on your ability to set the point of the needle close to where the thread comes up from the previous stitch. The more practice you have, the smaller the stitches get. Periodically check the backing to be sure the needle is going through, especially at intersecting lines.

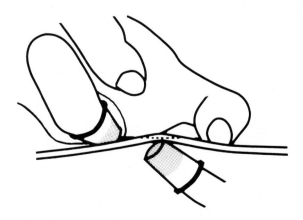

Figure E—Quilt with a running-stitch, taking 3 or 4 stitches at a time.

When you complete the outline of one detail in an appliqué and move to the next, do not knot and cut the thread. With the last stitch, push your needle into, but not through, the batting. Slide the needle in this concealed manner to the next-closest feature, where the needle surfaces.

When all details of the appliqué are quilted, or when you come to the end of a thread, don't knot the thread. Finish it by taking a back-stitch, page 9, through the second-to-last stitch. Punch the needle into the batting and pull the needle through a short distance from the stitching. Draw the needle through the top, tug and cut thread close, but not too close to fabric.

Quilt the way you marked the design on the top layer in diagonal lines. Go first in one direction, then the other. To avoid a lopsided result with pleats on the backing, do all quilting from the center out and from edge-to-edge. Quilt an entire line from the edge of the appliquéd square to the outside edge before you begin the next parallel line.

ADDING APPLIQUÉ TO BACK PIECE

When quilting is complete, turn the quilt over to the back piece. Pin on the appliqué, using the quilting outline as a guide. Baste in place from the center out.

The back of the appliqué is attached only to the back piece. It is not quilted but applied with a decorative buttonhole-stitch, page 10. Details of the front appliqué are stitched, but the back is only outlined along its outer edges.

TRIMMING BACK PIECE

Begin by basting 1/4 to 1/2 inch from the edge on all four sides. This secures fabric and accurately marks the backing. Trace around all sides with a pencil. Trim excess fabric according to the lines.

ADDING BIAS

The finishing step is to cover the raw edges with large, double-fold bias tape. For directions on making and attaching continuous bias, see page 6. If you prefer, use ready-made bias in a matching color.

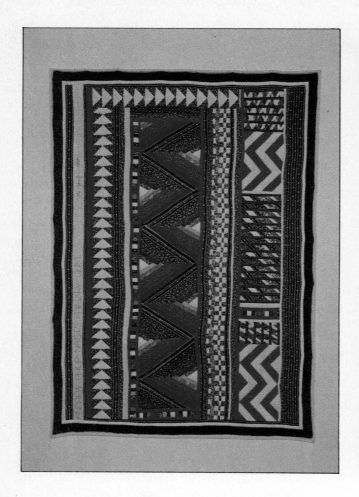

Andrew's Primary Quilt

This spectacular quilt top consists of almost 1,000 pieces and measures 42x60". It is a complex project intended by its maker to become an heirloom. Whether or not you choose to reproduce it, study the different piecing patterns in the quilt. You will find many ideas for your own heirloom quilt, which might be made from one or more of the patterns given below. See page 26 for Graphing a Pattern.

Instructions below correspond to the key. See Figure A. See the Appliqué Patchwork Quilts, page 26, and the section on Construction Terms, Techniques and Equipment, page 5, for more information on graphing, piecing and quilting procedures.

EQUIPMENT
- Pattern-making supplies, page 15
- Quilting needles. Short, hairpin needles, size 8 to 10, sometimes called betweens, see page 21.

- Ruler or yardstick, page 20
- No. 2 pencil for pale-color fabric
- White pencil or charcoal for dark-color fabric
- Water-solvent pen to mark quilting design. Test all water-solvent pens on scrap fabric before applying to quilt.
- Quilter's frame or large round or oval embroidery hoop
- Thimble
- Water sprayer for removing water-solvent ink, optional

MATERIALS
- Amount of fabric will vary, depending on the size of your quilt. Determine amounts before you begin by first planning your design on graph paper.
- Fabric for backing. Amount depends on the size of the quilt.
- 1 yard of 45-inch-wide fabric for bias
- Polyester thread for machine-stitching
- Cotton quilting thread with a glace finish
- Batting, page 18. Amount depends on the size of the quilt.

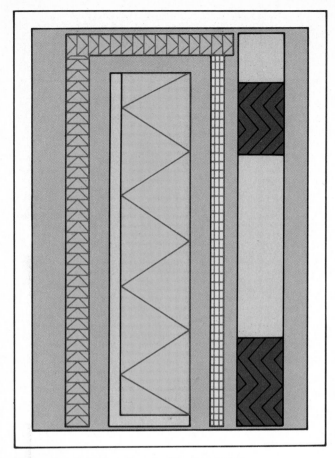

Figure A—Color key for clarification only:

One-piece strip

Seminole

Log cabin

Wild-goose chase

Streak o' lightning

Irish chain

LOG CABIN

The log-cabin design is a patchwork section usually built from a square. In the center is a small square. Longer strips are added to the sides in a particular order to make larger squares. This is a popular design. Variations of it can be found in most quilting books. Some books are listed in the *Bibliography,* page 158.

The shape of the finished patchwork section depends on the shape of the center. In addition to the square, you can use hexagons, triangles or diamonds. Other variations may be obtained by altering positions of light and dark fabric.

In this quilt, strips are sewn together to make two diamonds. The diamond is then cut in half.

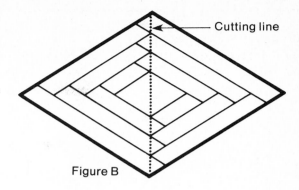

Figure B

See Figure B. Begin with the smallest diamond. Add strips on four sides to make larger diamonds. For cutting, tearing or piecing strips, see page 18.

To begin the sequence, sew a strip along one side. Iron and trim excess fabric that shows on the right-side. Sew a strip along the opposite side, iron and trim it. Continue sewing strips on opposite sides until you reach the desired size.

When diamond is finished, cut in half to make two triangles. Stitch sides of one triangle to next adjacent triangle. This pieced panel forms the center of the quilt. See photo. The common base of these diamonds is a one-piece strip extending the length of all four patchwork pieces. There are three kinds of strips in this quilt—one-piece, seminole and Irish chain.

ONE-PIECE STRIPS

A one-piece strip is the easiest to make. See the *Appliqué Patchwork Quilts,* page 26, for directions on how to make a one-piece strip.

SEMINOLE

The seminole is a strip of blocks in at least two contrasting colors. Some blocks are all one-piece and regular in size, such as the multicolored L-shape strip outlining the log-cabin constructions. These regular blocks can be presented in many shapes. In this quilt, there are strips of rectangles, squares and parallelograms. To set them off with depth and contrast, each seminole strip is bordered with one-piece strips.

Many blocks make up each strip in this quilt. In the L-shape seminole bordering the log-cabin section, there are 92 blocks. If you don't want as much detail in your quilt, you can create a similar effect by using fewer, larger blocks.

To make the blocks, use the same procedure as the larger patchwork block of the *Appliqué Patchwork Quilts.* See *Piecing,* page 27.

There is another way to piece seminole blocks and strips. The seminole sections above each streak o' lightning section are made by the technique of strip piecing.

Strip Piecing—Choose fabric in coordinated colors and prints. Wash, dry and iron fabric before cutting. Tear fabric along the straight grain in different widths. The widths used here range from 1 to 1-1/4 inches. Save one fabric to make the lattice. In this quilt, the lattice strips are the one-piece, blue-print bands alternating with the strip-piece bands. Lattice strips in a contrasting color add depth and distinction to the strip piecing. Cut all lattice strips the same width. In this case, the width is 1 inch.

Sew strips together in staggered positions, using colors randomly. Use the edge of the pressure foot as the seam-allowance guide. See Figure C. Each row is set off from the next about 1/2 inch. Iron seams toward the darker fabric.

Use a ruler to mark strips on the cloth. Cut cloth in strips according to the dotted lines. See Figure C. Cut and sew these strips together with the reserved lattice strips. See Figure D.

IRISH CHAIN

The Irish chain consists of three strips. It is made from two contrasting colors. Make strips the same way as for the seminole and log-cabin blocks. Alternate light blocks with dark blocks. Begin the first and third strip with a light square and the middle strip with a dark square. In this quilt, a fourth strip begins with a dark square. It was set apart from the chain by a long, one-piece strip.

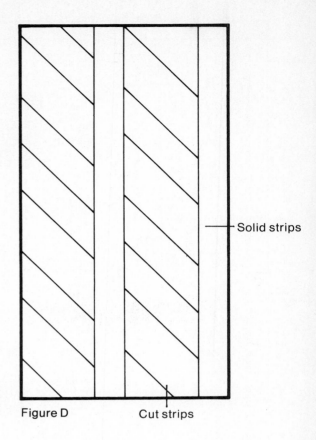

Solid strips

Figure D   Cut strips

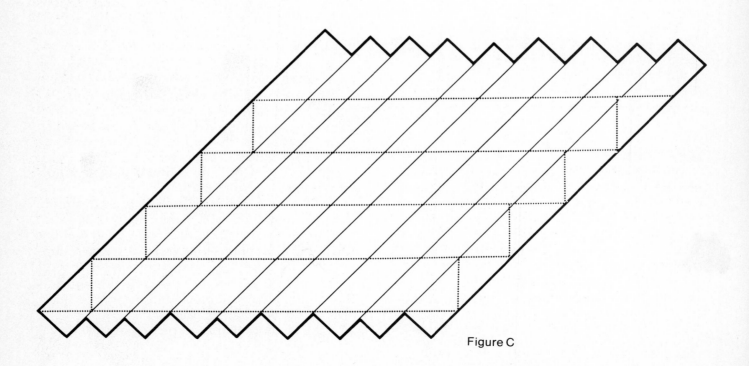

Figure C

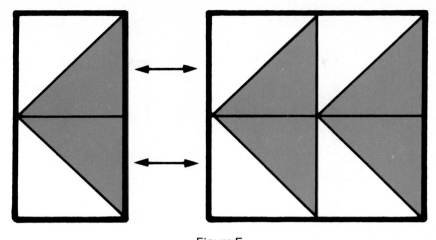

Figure E

WILD-GOOSE CHASE

This four-piece pattern is made from scrap triangles. See page 16 for directions on how to construct a basic unit. For the chase, cut an equal number of triangles in light and dark colors. In this quilt there are 90 of each. Place two bicolored squares side-by-side to form the larger triangle.

To piece the strip together, lay one block under another block. Points of the larger triangle face in the same direction. Pin and sew the seams together, then press the seams to one side. Continue until all strips are finished. See Figure E.

STREAK O' LIGHTNING

Like the wild-goose chase, this pattern consists of blocks made from two triangles in contrasting colors. Arrange blocks in an alternating light-dark pattern, as shown on the quilt. See the close-up photograph on page 30.

Sew blocks together in horizontal bands rather than strips, then sew bands together. For variation, work some one-piece blocks in a solid color with the diagonal blocks to create other patterns.

SELF-FINISHED EDGING FROM BACKING

This quilt is bound with its own backing. Cut the backing 1-1/2 inches larger than the quilt top on all sides. When quilting is finished, bring the backing forward. Fold edges under, and stitch by hand or machine. For information on mitering corners, see page 14.

TUBE FOR MOUNTING

This mounting method uses a fabric-tube casing in the same color as the backing. It is a good method to use if you want to use the quilt and hang it. Casings made from strips allow wood to rub against the backing of the quilt. Rubbing can damage a quilt. With this method, fabric keeps the wood from rubbing the quilt.

Cut a 3-inch strip on the fold of fabric. Make the strip the desired length and add a 1/2-inch seam allowance. End the tube about 1 inch inside the edging on each side. This keeps the casing from showing on the right-side. On the short ends of the 6-inch strip, turn under a 1/4-inch seam. Press and stitch the seam by hand or machine. Fold the strip in half across the width, with wrong-sides together. Match raw edges, pin and stitch the entire length. Turn the tube right-side out and press.

Center and pin the tube to the top of the quilt. Pin it about 1/2 inch down from the top edge. Stitch along the long edge, leaving the short ends open.

Insert a sanded wood strip or dowel in the tube that has been cut to the desired length. If you want to use a less-visible method, cut the wood longer than the casing, but shorter than the quilt. Near each end, add small screw eyes or drill holes for hanging.

Accessories for Home and Travel

Setting up the nursery is more than a decorating challenge. Color-coordinating and choosing themes is fun, but you must also consider expense, practicality and durability of the items you need. Accessories for baby will be used for a short period of time, but they are used consistently and soiled repeatedly.

In this section, you will find some unusual approaches to making projects. Bumper pads are designed to look as good after machine-washing as before. The versatile diaper storage and backpack can easily by adapted for other uses when baby is out of diapers. Other items, such as covers for the car seat and a changing-table pad, include instructions for making your own patterns because these projects vary in size.

Most projects can be made less expensively than if you purchase them ready made. Many things can be made from materials around the house, such as washcloths, sheets and fabric scraps.

Any project can be color-coordinated. You can even adapt it to a particular theme!

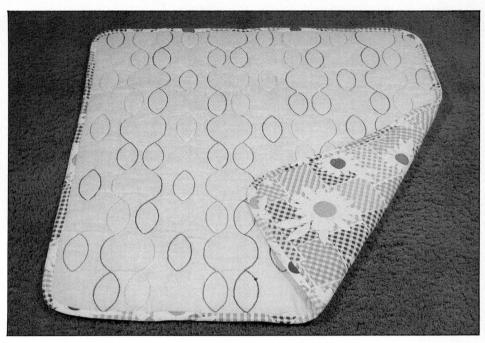

Reversible Play Mat

Dress up an ordinary mattress pad with embroidery. This area-defining play mat can be used as a nap mat or a play pad, at home or when traveling. It is an area-defining mat and will be useful long into childhood.

This mat is as easy to make as it looks. Buy a crib or youth-bed mattress pad. If necessary, cut it to a desired size. This one is 36x38". For the backing, cut a tablecloth, sheet or piece of fabric 2 inches larger than the pad. Baste the pad and fabric together.

Mark and trim the pad and fabric the same way as a quilt backing. Sew pieces together around the edges and add bias. Another way is to use the backing as bias. See page 6. If you're making a ruffle, page 17, sew the pad, ruffle and backing together in one operation.

Changing Pad

Decorate an inexpensive pad purchased at a store. Use an appliqué and a few yards of ready-made ruffles or double-edge bias tape. Add two sets of ties on one short end of the pad. You can roll up the pad and tie it or use ties for hanging. If you need it, you have a pillow to keep baby from rolling over. This pad is great for travel or in the nursery—as a changing pad or a wall hanging!

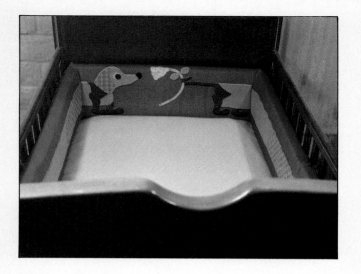

7-1/2 inches, the width of the cover should be 9-1/2 inches. If the depth of your foam is *more* than 1 inch, add 1/8 inch to the width measurement for every 1/2 inch of thickness. If 7-1/2-inch foam is 1-1/2 inches thick, add 1/8 inch to the 9-1/2-inch measurement, for 9-5/8 inches.

For the four middle sections, add 1 inch to the length of foam to allow for 1/2-inch seams when sewing sections into a strip. If your crib is standard size, each section will measure 26 inches.

For the two end sections, add 2 inches to the length of the foam for the cover. This allows enough fabric to make openings. For the standard crib, each section will measure 27 inches.

Prepare to cut three sections at a time. Fold the fabric selvage to the width measurement, with right-sides together. Divide the folded length into sections according to your measurements. See Figure A.

Bumper Pads

These practical bumper pads can be decorated with a dachshund or other appliqué. The single-tube pad cover has openings at both ends for easy removal of six foam blocks. Each block is covered with plastic and can be wiped clean. The cover can be machine-washed.

EQUIPMENT
- **Sewing supplies**
- **1/4-inch eyelet hole-puncher kit**
- **Fabric marker, page 20**
- **Heavy cardboard or small cutting board for hammering grommets**
- **Embroidery hoop, optional**

MATERIALS
- **Foam. See instructions for measuring amount.**
- **2-3/4 yards of 45-inch-wide fabric for covers and ties**
- **2-3/4 yards of 45-inch-wide plastic for covering foam**
- **6 to 8 sets of snaps, Velcro or other touch-and-close fasteners**
- **Fabric for appliqué. Amounts vary, depending on how many different fabrics you use.**
- **Iron-on interfacing. Amount varies, depending on the size of your appliqués.**

CUTTING AND STITCHING BUMPER-PAD COVERS

The average inside measurements of a crib are 28x52". Using 1-1/2-inch foam, cut six pieces 25x6 or 25x7-1/2".

Six fabric sections must be sewn in a tube to cover the foam. Each section is the same width. Determine the width of the cover by adding 2 inches to the height of the foam. If your foam is

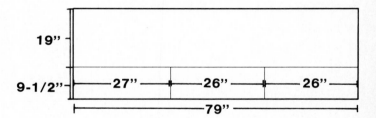

Figure A

Cut the fabric. Pin the sections in a strip, with right-sides together. Begin and end with a 27-inch section. Stitch the six pieces together in one continuous tube with 1/2-inch seams. Press seams open.

ADDING APPLIQUÉS

Enlarge appliqués according to the pattern. See Figure B. Cut 10 rectangles that are each 4x13" from fabric for the body. Add iron-on interfacing to the wrong-side of the fabric. With a pencil or fabric marker, trace pattern shapes on the interfacing side. Cut out, adding 1/4 inch for finishing edges. Turn and baste or pin together the raw edges of each piece. When finished, set pieces aside. Iron the bumper cover strip free of wrinkles.

The head, tail and flower pieces are basted on the third section of the strip at either end. Determine the correct placement of these pieces on the background by inserting with pins and pinning a foam block in position. Indicate with pins where the pieces need to be sewn, then remove foam.

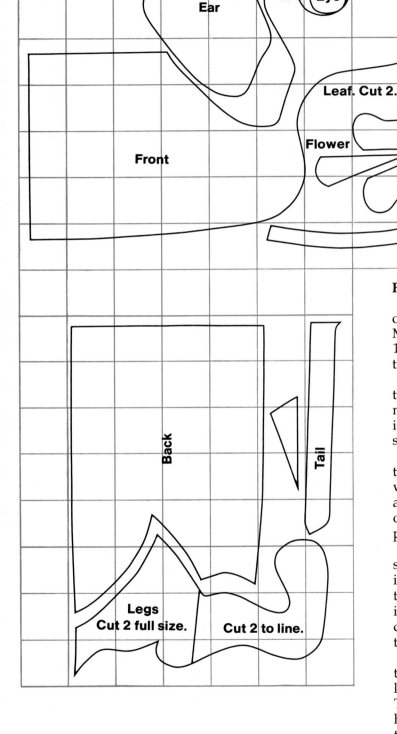

Ear

Eye

Nose

Leaf. Cut 2.

Flower

Front

Stem

Back

Tail

Legs
Cut 2 full size.

Cut 2 to line.

Figure B—Cut sections for tubes three at a time. You will need two 27-inch tubes and four 27-inch tubes.

FINISHING BUMPER PADS

With right-sides together, fold the long strip of fabric in half lengthwise to form a tube. Match raw edges, pin and stitch the length with 1/2-inch seams. Turn right-side out, and press the tube.

Wrap each foam section with a piece of plastic, the way you would wrap a box with paper. To make removal less difficult later when the cover is soiled, use only a small amount of tape to secure the plastic.

To make openings at each end of the fabric tube, press raw edges under 1/2 inch to the wrong-side. Fold under another 1/2 inch, press and hem. There are similarities between these openings and the opening for the *Padded Sheets*, page 50.

Find the correct position for snaps and ties for securing the bumper pads to the crib. First, insert the plastic-covered foam cushions in the tube. Use seam lines as guide lines for positioning the foam. Next, put the pads in the crib and check the places to add ties. Ties secure the pads to the sides of the crib.

With a fabric marker, indicate positions for ties with a small dot. Remove the foam. Add eyelets for ties according to instructions on your kit. To keep from tearing underlying fabric, slip heavy cardboard or a small cutting board between layers of the tube while hammering grommets together. Sew snaps at each opening.

Cut fabric for six ties, each 16x2''. For making ties, see page 18. Slip ties through grommets and put the foam in the tube.

MAKING A PATTERN

Trace the vinyl pad from your car seat. Paper is sufficient for this purpose, but you'll be tailoring the pattern to fit your car seat. It may be better to use an old mattress pad. Add 1-1/2 inches around the edge when tracing the car seat pad. Replace the pad in the car seat when finished.

Next, modify this traced outline as shown in Figure A. Cut out the pattern. You will be sewing two seams on the bottom of the seat.

Fit the cut-out paper or mattress piece in your car seat. Make any necesssary adjustments. You may have to extend seams a couple of inches so they fit the back of the seat. If your car seat has a padded shield that slips over the baby, slip it in place during this fitting interfere with the attachment of the shield. Fabric may interfere with the attachment of the shield and need to be trimmed.

With the paper or pad pattern in the seat, wrap tissue paper or fabric around the back of the car seat. This makes a pattern for the back edge piece. Pin paper to the upper edges of the seat pattern, as shown in Figure B. Pin darts at the top corners of the back pattern piece to make the cover fit.

When the two pieces are securely in place, trim around the top and side edges of the back piece. It will take the shape of the seat. Fold the bottom of the paper to the desired hem length. The belt holes are not marked until the project is almost finished. See *Adding Belt Holes* on next page.

Car-Seat Cover

There are many different types of car-restraint safety seats, each made in a different style. This project will help you make a cover for your particular model. In addition to making the pattern, you can personalize it.

EQUIPMENT
- Sewing supplies
- Fabric markers, page 20
- Tissue paper or newspaper for making pattern
- Embroidery supplies
- Safety blade for making belt holes, optional

MATERIALS
- Fabric amount varies, depending on the size of your car seat. See the section on Making a Pattern, top right.
- Mattress pad or other quilted fabric
- 1 yard of 45-inch-wide fabric for the back piece
- Bias tape
- Iron-on transfers or other decorations
- 1/2-inch elastic. Amount depends on pattern.
- Ruffle, page 17, optional

CUTTING AND SEWING

Unpin the front pattern from the back piece. Remove pins or basting-stitches from seams. Lay the seat pattern on the wrong-side of your quilted material. Pin as close to the edges of the pattern as possible. Cut the pad or other quilted fabric, then baste the edges so layers don't separate as you work on them. Baste seams on the seat of the pad. Before stitching seams, put the pad in the car seat to check the fit.

With the new pad in the car seat, cut the back piece from the fabric. For tailoring purposes, pin the fabric to the pad as you did the pattern pieces. Pin darts in the back piece. Pin a hem that will be 3/4 inch wide when sewn. This becomes casing for elastic, if it is needed, to make the back piece fit more securely. See page 13 for information on hems and page 9 for adding a casing and elastic.

Remove the two pieces from the car seat and separate them. Set your sewing machine on the longest stitch. Sew seams on the mattress pad before removing basting-stitches. If you are personalizing the car seat with a child's name, you can do it now or when you finish.

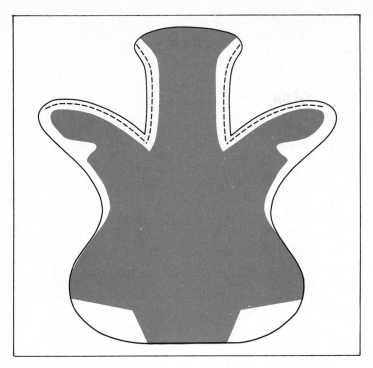

Figure A—Car-seat pad molds to curves of seat. See shaded area. Cover can be simplified. See overall shape.

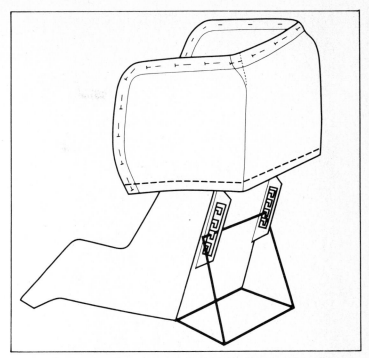

Figure B—Allow some slack, so back edge piece doesn't fit tightly. Leave enough material for 1-inch seam allowance.

With a smaller machine-stitch, sew darts on the back piece. Fold the raw edges under 1/4 inch and press. Fold under 1/4 inch again, press and machine- or hand-stitch.

Make a ruffle at this point, if you're adding one. See page 17. With right-sides together, pin the back fabric piece to the front fabric piece. Place the ruffle in the middle. Baste the three layers together and turn right-side out. If necessary, make adjustments. If you are not adding a ruffle, with right-sides together, pin the front fabric piece to the back fabric piece. Place the cover in the car seat to check the fit.

Remove the cover from the seat and turn it inside out. Using your sewing machine, stitch the layers together. Remove the basting stitch and turn right-side out.

To finish the bottom and side edges of the padded seat, purchase or make a bias strip 2 inches wide. See page 6. Attach bias to the back part of the cover with a machine stitch. Sew it to the front by hand or machine.

ADDING BELT HOLES AND ELASTIC

When the cover is finished, put it in the car seat, and mark belt holes. With the safety blade or large needle, enter the slots through the back of the car seat. Make a series of lines on the mattress pad that can be connected with a pencil.

Remove the cover from the car seat, and cut lines with scissors. Measure and cut two pieces

of bias the length of the slit, plus 1/2 inch. Fold under raw edges of all sides to the wrong-side 1/4 inch and press. Reinforce the sides with a double line of stitches. Attach bias tape to the tops and bottom of each slit, as shown in Figure C. See page 6 for attaching bias and page 7 for finishing buttonholes.

To help keep the cover in place, attach ties made of stitched bias tape to the sides. Place the cover in the car seat. Mark where to add ties to the edge of the cover. The bias tape ties around the frame to help keep the cover on the seat. Some car seats have two places ties can be used. Other car seats have four places to attach ties.

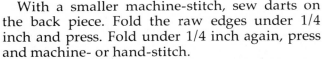

Figure C—When attaching bias, reinforce sides with double row of stitches.

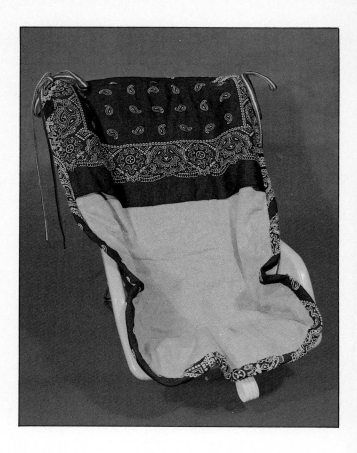

Fitted
Infant-Seat Cover

Like the fitted car-seat cover, the fitted infant-seat cover uses a mattress pad as the outside fabric. Following the directions given for the Car-Seat Cover, page 38, you can use another prequilted fabric. You can even quilt your own, using a mattress pad as the middle layer.

Denim
Infant-Seat Cover

This quilted cover, tied with yarn and trimmed with bandannas, is sturdy and reversible. It can also be used as a changing pad.

EQUIPMENT
- Sewing supplies
- Fabric marker, page 20

MATERIALS
- 1 yard of 45-inch-wide denim
- 2 bandannas
- 1 large mattress pad or other filling, page 18
- Shoelaces or other trim, optional

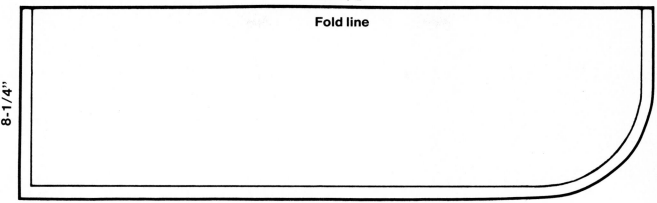

26-1/2"

Fold line

8-1/4"

Figure A—For pattern, make rectangle 16-1/2x26-1/2". Fold in half lengthwise and round off edge on one corner. Start curve about 5 inches from bottom edge on each side. See the *Diaper Backpack*, page 44, for instructions on rounding corners.

QUILTING PAD

Make your own pattern to fit your infant seat. Cut out the pattern pieces according to the pattern shown in Figure A. Prepare the fabric as shown on page 16. Cut the mattress pad or filling the size of the pattern. Cut denim front and back pieces 1 inch larger.

Place the mattress pad between the front and back pieces, with the right-side of the denim facing you. Baste the layers in place. See page 6. Tie layers at random with yarn, page 19. When tying is complete, trim the edges of the denim to the size of the mattress pad.

ADDING TRIM

Iron one bandanna, then fold it over the top of the infant-seat cover. Baste it in place, page 9. Sew the bandanna in place by hand or with the longest stitch on your machine. See Figure B. When stitching and trimming are complete, make bias from the second bandanna, page 6. Sew bias around the edges of the cover.

If adding decorative shoelaces, remove plastic ends. Stitch them in place by hand.

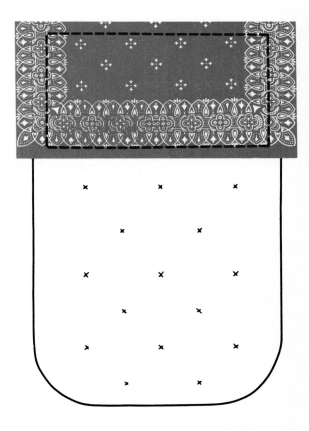

Figure B—When bandanna is stitched, trim edges to match denim pieces and middle layer.

Pad Cover

Sew a terry-cloth patchwork of washcloths. You can use colorful hand or dish towels. Patches in larger sizes are less expensive. You may prefer to use a solid piece of fabric. These simple instructions can also be used to make a pad cover for a playpen.

EQUIPMENT
- Sewing supplies
- Fabric marker, page 20
- Template, see Make Patchwork Top in next column

MATERIALS
- Amount of fabric varies, depending on the size of your pad. See the section on Taking Measurements above right.
- 3/4- or 1-inch-thick foam. Buy enough to cover the inside of the dressing table or playpen.
- Enough plastic to cover foam

Or
- 1 purchased pad to fit your changing table
- 1 strip of Velcro, 4 to 5 inches long

Or
- 3 or 4 Velcro snaps or other snaps

TAKING MEASUREMENTS
If you are covering foam, measure the inside bottom of the dressing table or playpen. Cut foam 3/4 to 1 inch narrower, depending on the thickness of the plastic and fabric to cover. If covering a purchased pad, you may have to trim edges to get the covered pad to fit the dressing table or playpen.

If your foam is not plastic-covered, you need to determine how much plastic is needed. Measure the width of the foam. Double this measurement, and add 3 inches. Cut plastic the same length as the foam and as wide as the doubled width, plus 3 inches.

To determine how much fabric is needed for a plastic-covered pad, measure the top and bottom separately. For the top cover, measure the foam and add 2 inches to the length and 2 inches to the width measurements. For the bottom cover, add 8 inches to the length and 2 inches to the width measurements.

COVERING FOAM
Fold plastic in half across the width. Stitch a 1/4-inch seam across the width, making a tube. Turn the tube right-side out and place foam inside.

COVERING PAD
Begin on the bottom cover. Cut the fabric in half lengthwise to make a lap. This makes removal of the foam easy. Fold raw edges under 1/2 inch to the wrong-side along one long edge of each bottom piece. Press. Fold under 1/2 inch to form a finished seam and press again. Stitch 1/8 inch from inside edge, as shown in Figure A.

Use a one-piece top or make a patchwork top. See below. Put the top and two bottom pieces together, with right-sides facing. The stitched folds are in the center of the cover and overlap one another. See Figure B. Stitch a 1/2-inch seam around the cover, and turn it right-side out. See Figure C. Add Velcro fasteners to each side of the lap so it can be opened and closed. This joins the cover more securely over the slippery plastic-covered foam. Place foam inside.

MAKE PATCHWORK TOP
Make a template that will use as much of the terry cloth as possible. The washcloths or hand towels may not be the same size. The washcloths used in this example were about 11-inches square. To use all of them, a 9x4-1/2" template was made. This made it possible to cut two 9x4-1/2" pieces from each washcloth.

Sew the pieces in strips, with right-sides together. See Figure D. Stitch the strips in rows, with right-sides together. For a pad cover, assemble separate patchwork pieces for the top and bottom. Treat the patchwork as a solid piece of fabric. The pad cover is made the same way as described above.

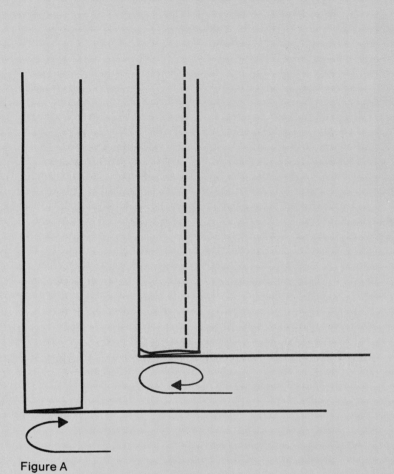

Figure A

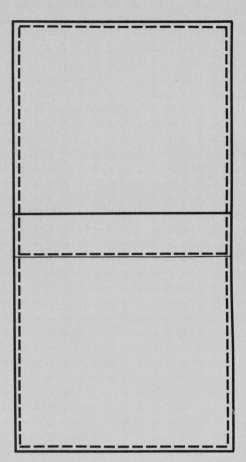

Figure C

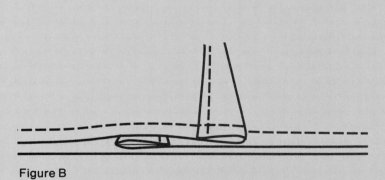

Figure B

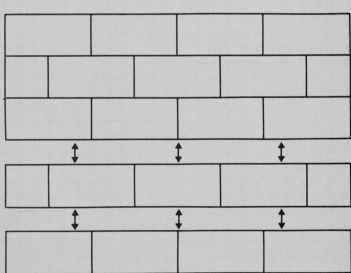

Figure D—For staggered rows, make every other row irregular. Cut one terry rectangle in two. Sew half to each end of strip.

Diaper Backpack

Unlike a cumbersome diaper bag, this plastic-lined backpack is out of the way, yet convenient. Long after baby has grown, the bag will continue to be useful. Note the easy-access pockets.

EQUIPMENT
- Sewing supplies
- Scissors, page 19
- Pinking shears, page 20
- Measuring tape or yardstick, page 20
- Pencil
- Grommet tool
- Candle, for searing
- 1-1/2 yards of paper for pattern, page 15
- French curve, optional

MATERIALS
- 1-1/2 yards of 45-inch-wide, preshrunk denim
- 1 piece of plastic, 32x22''
- 2 bandannas
- 2 yards of 1-1/2- to 2-inch-wide webbing for straps
- 4 D-rings, to fit webbing
- 6 grommets
- 1 pocket removed from old jeans
- 1 pair shoelaces

MAKING PATTERN
Make pattern pieces according to the pattern shown in Figure A. Make one denim front-back piece 32x14'', two denim side pieces 13-1/2x7'' and two denim pocket pieces 8-1/2x7''. Make one plastic front-back piece 31x14'' and two plastic pieces 12-1/2x6-1/2''. Make one flap out of denim and one flap from the bandanna. Make them each 14x15''. Cut webbing in two 15-inch and two 19-inch lengths. If you have an old pair of jeans, remove a pocket from them.

ATTACHING POCKETS
Begin working with the side pockets. Trim decorative borders from one bandanna. Fold the raw edges of the bandanna border under 1/4 inch and press. Fold under 1/4 inch again, press and machine- or hand-stitch. Pin bandanna borders to the right-side of the denim pocket. Match edges with the top of the pocket.

Fold 1/4 inch on the raw edges of the pocket tops to the wrong-side of the fabric and press. Fold the raw edges under 1/4 inch and press.

Stitch the top and bottom edges of the pocket to secure hems. Sew the other pocket the same way. When hemming is complete, pin one

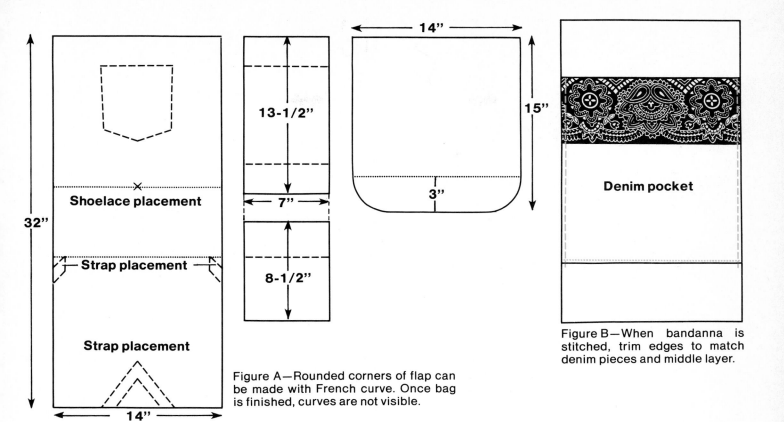

Shoelace placement

Strap placement

Strap placement

32"

14"

13-1/2"

7"

8-1/2"

14"

15"

3"

Figure A—Rounded corners of flap can be made with French curve. Once bag is finished, curves are not visible.

Denim pocket

Figure B—When bandanna is stitched, trim edges to match denim pieces and middle layer.

pocket to each denim side piece. The wrong-side of the pocket is pinned to the right-side of the side piece. Baste the sides and stitch the bottom of the pocket to the denim. See Figure B. Pin the pocket from the jeans to the front piece 3 inches from the top. See photo on page 44.

SEWING BAG AND LINING

After pockets are added, finish making the denim bag. Begin by sewing a shoelace to the bottom of the bag. See Figure A for placement.

Prepare to add nylon straps. Sear the end of each strap to prevent unraveling. See page 18 for information on searing.

Straps are added to the back piece and stitched in the seam when side panels are added. Pin the straps with the ends positioned as indicated on the pattern. See Figure C. Next, pin both side panels to the back piece, with right-sides together. When you pin sections together, line up raw edges accurately.

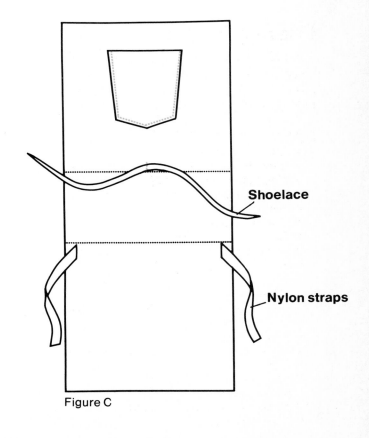

Shoelace

Nylon straps

Figure C

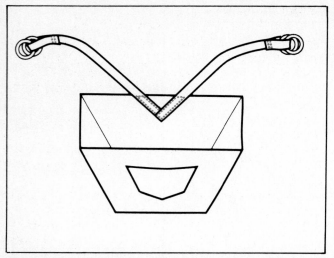

Figure D—Fold tops of bottom straps inward. They will be in correct position when bag is turned right-side out.

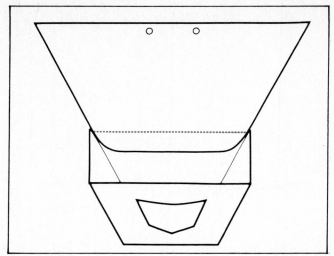

Figure E

Stitch a 1/2-inch seam along each side panel from top to bottom. Hold fabric taut as you ease it into the machine. When you reach the bottom of the seam, leave the needle in the denim. Lift the pressure foot, turn the fabric and continue sewing.

Match the bottom edges of the side panel to the edges of the front piece. Pin and stitch in place.

After you sew all the way around, reinforce the seams with straps by stitching them again. Clip corners, page 18, trim seams with pinking shears and turn the denim bag right-side out.

When the denim bag is finished, make a plastic bag the same way, except without straps. Turn the plastic bag right-side out so raw edges will be concealed when you slip this bag inside the denim bag.

Turn under 1/4 inch of the top edge of the denim bag. Press. Fold under 1/4 inch again to form a finished edge. Press again. Place the plastic bag inside the denim bag. Slip the raw edge of the plastic under the pressed denim edge. Center the 19-inch strap ends in a V-shape 4 inches from the top. Stitch in place. Thread one D-ring on each strap. Fold end over rings and stitch. See Figure D for both these steps.

Stitch the bandanna flap piece to the denim flap piece. With right-sides together, stitch a 1/2-inch seam around the edges. Leave a 5-inch opening between the rounded corners. Clip corners, turn right-side out and stitch the opening closed.

Attach the rounded flap end inside the bag on the wrong-side of the back piece. Place it so it covers the strap ends. See Figure E. Stitch through the flap and back piece.

Use a grommet tool to put two grommets in the flap and two at the top of each side piece. See the photograph. To close the bag, put the shoelace through the grommets and pull.

MAKING BAG

Enlarge the pattern, using the technique described on page 12. Cut out the pattern piece according to the pattern shown in Figure A. Cut two pieces on the fold, according to markings on the pattern. Sew the appliqué on the front piece, page 5.

After the appliqué is sewn on, pin the bag with right-sides together. Stitch from dot to dot, as shown in Figure A. Reinforce stitches at the openings. Clip corners, page 18, and turn the bag right-side out.

Fold under remaining raw edges on the top and sides under 1/4 inch and press. Fold under 1/4 inch again, press and machine- or hand-stitch. Pull top edges of bag over handles, and slip-stitch to the wrong-side of bag, page 13.

Nursery Laundry Bag

Make this bag and appliqué it with a character or setting created by a child. This cat was inspired by the felt-tip drawing in the collection of Children's Embroidery-Hoop Projects, page 115. The artwork has irregular lines, so imperfections became part of the design. Draw original shapes on the fabric the way you see them.

EQUIPMENT
- Enlarging supplies for the bag, page 12
- Sewing supplies

MATERIALS
- 1 pair of handbag handles with a 9-inch slot for bag attachment
- 1-1/2 yards of 36-inch-wide fabric for bag
- Fabric scraps for appliqué

Or
- 1 premade appliqué

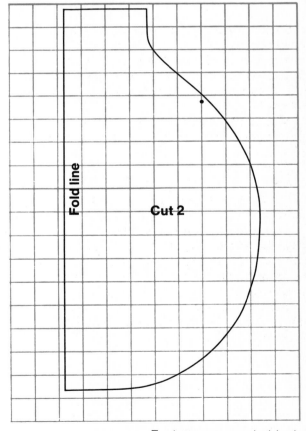

Fold line

Cut 2

Each square equals 1 inch.

Figure A—Measure your handle before beginning. If necessary, adjust the top opening of your pattern.

Hanging Diaper Stacker

Here's an inexpensive way to turn ceiling area into storage space. When baby's out of diapers, stackers can be used for other purposes.

EQUIPMENT
- Scissors, page 20
- 16 rubber bands

Or

- 16 pieces of yarn

MATERIALS
- 96 yards of cord or other macramé material
- 3 stackable plastic storage bins
- 12 wood or ceramic beads, 1 to 2 inches wide
- 1 brass ring, 2 to 3 inches

MAKING STACKER

Cut eight 12-yard pieces of cord, and fold each in half. Attach cord to the brass ring at the half-way point. Tie with a reversed double-half hitch. See Figure A. This leaves 16 cords hanging from the ring. Wind the end of each cord loosely in a loop around your hand and secure with a rubber band or piece of yarn. See Figure B. This reduces the length of the cord so it can be handled more easily.

Start with the four cords on the outside of the ring. Tie 12 inches of square knots—about 24 knots. See page 100 for information on tying square knots. Keep the two center cords tight as you tie. About 12 inches below your last square knot, begin tying another foot of square knots. Total length will be 36 inches. Repeat this with the four cords on the other side of the ring.

With the four cords in the center, start a length of square knots 12 inches from the ring. Tie 12 inches of square knots. Repeat this with the four remaining cords.

Put matching knotted lengths through opposite corners of the first storage basket. Slide a bead up each group of four cords until it reaches the bottom of the storage-basket leg. Keeping your basket level, tie an overhand knot below each bead. See Figure C of the *Crib Exerciser*, page 99. This will hold the basket in place. Repeat this procedure for each basket.

Finish by tying a square knot below each of the bottom overhand knots. Trim bottoms so about 12 inches of cord is left. Unravel cord ends to make a tassel.

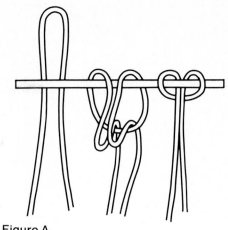

Figure A

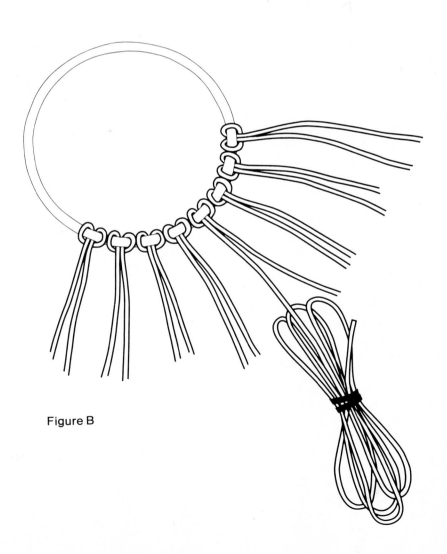

Figure B

Padded Sheets

This project can be adapted for any mattress you want to cover. One side is padded, so a fitted mattress pad under the reversible sheet is unnecessary.

EQUIPMENT
- Sewing supplies
- Marker for quilt lines, page 20

MATERIALS
- Amount of fabric varies, depending on the size of your mattress. See the section below on Making Top.
- Fabric to make 2 ties, each 12 inches long
- Lace or other trim, optional

MAKING TOP
The padded sheet in the photograph fits a port-a-crib mattress and measures 38x24''. Cut the mattress pad to the measurement of the mattress.

To find the amount of fabric needed for the top piece, add 3 inches to the length measurement and 1 inch to the width. This port-a-crib mattress top piece measures 41x25''.

Choose a fabric with a contrasting border, print or check, or use a plain sheet. As an alternative, consider making it from prequilted fabric. It may be more expensive but it will save steps and time.

Draw diagonal lines on the pad with a marker, as shown in Figure A. With marks facing you, baste the pad to the wrong-side of the top piece. Baste around the pad, 1/2 inch from the edge, along the two long sides and one short side. See page 6 for basting.

To quilt the pad, follow the lines on the pad, and begin stitching in the middle. If adding lace or trim, do it *after* machine-quilting is complete, before the top piece is machine-stitched to the backing piece.

For the backing piece, add 3 inches to the length of the mattress. For the width, measure the depth of the mattress at the side and add 1/2 inch. If the side measures 1-3/4 inches on a small mattress, add 1/2 inch for a total of 2-1/4 inches.

The backing piece needs to cover the sides of the mattress. If the side is 2-1/4 inches, double the measurement to 4-1/2 inches. Add it to the width measurement. The backing piece for a mattress measuring 38x24'' is 41x28-1/2''. Cut a worn sheet for this purpose or use another washable fabric.

MAKING BOTTOM
Place the bottom piece right-side down on the mattress. Leave an equal amount of fabric on two long sides and one short one. The second

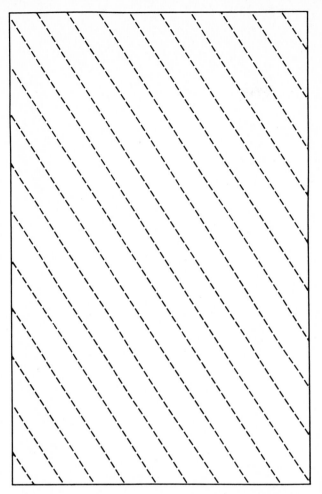

Figure A—Begin at center and draw diagonal lines from one corner to another. Parallel lines are 2 inches apart.

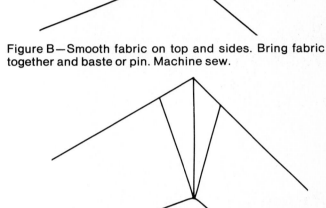

Figure B—Smooth fabric on top and sides. Bring fabric together and baste or pin. Machine sew.

Figure C—Press seams open.

shorter side needs extra fabric for the opening.

Work first with the sides to be covered. Pull up the material and miter the corners as illustrated in Figures B and C. Remove bottom piece from mattress. With right-sides together, baste and sew the top to the bottom with 1/2-inch seams. Sew along the three sides, and turn right-side out.

FINISHING OPENING

Make ties and stitch the raw edges of the top piece to the wrong-side of the fabric with a 1/4-inch seam. Repeat this for the back piece. Place mattress inside cover before measuring the hem.

Beginning with the top piece, pin the hem of the flap so it covers the open end of the mattress. Repeat for the bottom piece. Attach ties when stitching hems. See Figure D.

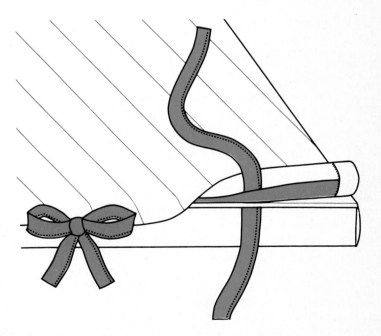

Figure D—Extra material on sides is folded under flap and secured with ties.

Braided
Rocker Cover

Make durable, padded covers for a rocking chair, highchair or other baby furniture by braiding leftover scraps. The only stitching needed is to prepare the strips for braiding and then to sew one end of the strip to the next. Four-stranded braiding involves simple sewing and weaving.

EQUIPMENT
- Scissors, page 20
- 4 small-to-medium-size safety pins
- Needle for hand-sewing, page 20
- T-pins, page 20
- Knotting board, page 20, optional

MATERIALS
- Fabric scraps in cotton, synthetic or blends
- Thread to match fabrics

PREPARING STRIPS
Strips can be cut on the lengthwise or crosswise grain. Cut or tear 2-inch-wide strips in varying lengths. Make them each 1 to 2 yards long. Cut strips different lengths so the stress on the fabric occurs at different points on each strand. Strips of shorter scraps can be sewn together for longer lengths.

After cutting strips, sew together the shorter scraps. Fold the raw edges of each strip to the center of the wrong-side. Iron the folds, then baste or stitch strips closed on the machine as you fold. Refold along the middle to hide raw edges. See page 18.

MAKING CENTER BRAID
The interlocking braiding begins with a center, three-strand braided strip. To estimate the size to make your center, subtract your planned width from its length, and add 1 inch. If the back of your chair measures 16x12'', the length of your three-strand center braid will be 5 inches. The extra inch provides an allowance when the center braid turns over itself as the fourth strip is added. See Figure A.

If you are working with a square area, such as the seat of a chair, you will make a round pad. You will need a center braid only a few inches long because the interlocking strand needs to be added sooner to make the circular shape.

Select three strips of different lengths for the center braid. Sew these strips together at one end and keep the center strip straight. As you begin braiding it, have another person hold the stitched end or attach the end to a knotting board with a T-pin. Braid the strips to their measured length, page 7. Weave strips tautly, but not so tight as to keep the pad from lying flat.

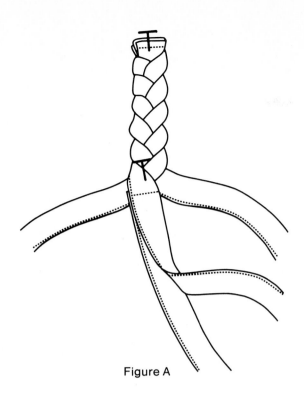

Figure A

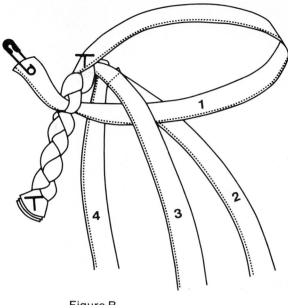

Figure B

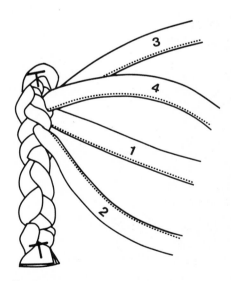

Figure C

BRAIDING WITH FOUR STRANDS

When the center strip is braided, sew the fourth strip under the last crossover of the original three. See Figure A. Attach a safety pin to the end of each strip.

Begin braiding with four strands in the following manner. In your mind, number each strip from right to left, 1 through 4. Begin by weaving 1 over 2, under 3, over 4 and through the adjacent loop of the center braid. See Figure B. Strip 2 becomes strip 1. Repeat the process of weaving over, under, over and through the adjacent loop of the center braid. See Figure C. Do the same when strip 3 becomes strip 1. Except for rounding corners and adding new strips, continue in the same uninterrupted sequence.

When rounding corners, the adjacent loop is the one you just brought the last strip through. To avoid puckering the pad, bring the next strip through this same loop. Occasionally the same loop is used for as many as three strips before the succeeding loop is adjacent to the next interlocking strip. Follow the path set by your center braid.

Stitch new strips as they are needed, with right-sides together. Raw edges face the same side. Seams can usually be hidden or worked to appear on the underside of the pad. When the correct size is achieved, cut the end of each strip 1 to 2 inches from the end.

Weave raw edges to the underside. Hand-stitch them in place. Tie the finished pads to the rocker or other furniture with leftover strips.

Clothing and Necessities

Simple lines are used for the baby clothes in these projects. Clothes are easy and inexpensive to make. Many were designed for someone without a lot of spare time.

Clothes allow for plenty of growing room. The *Pinafore*, page 64, with its open sides, and the *Kimono Jacket*, page 69, with its open front, allow baby to wear the garment for a long time. The easy, one-size-fits-all *Swim Poncho*, page 55, can be worn from infancy through toddlerhood.

Baby clothes don't take much fabric. You may have enough scraps to add accessories to an outfit. Included in this section are simple patterns for accessories, such as *Booties*, page 73, *Bibs*, pages 77 and 80, and the *Sunbonnet*, page 78.

INFANT SIZES

Size	Pounds	Size	Pounds
0 to 3 months	Up to 10	Small	10 to 16
3 to 6 months	8 to 14	Medium	16 to 22
6 to 9 months	12 to 18	Large	20 to 26
12 months	18 to 24	Extra-Large	24 to 30
18 months	22 to 28		
24 months	26 to 34		

TODDLER SIZES

Size	Waist	Height	Weight
2T	20-1/2 to 21 inches	32 to 34 inches	27 to 29 pounds
3T	21 to 21-1/2 inches	35 to 37 inches	32 to 34 pounds
4T	21-1/2 to 22 inches	38 to 40 inches	36 to 38 pounds

Swim Poncho

With one size fitting all, baby can wear this terry-cloth cover-up year after year.

EQUIPMENT
- **Enlarging supplies, page 12**
- **Sewing supplies**

MATERIALS
- **3/8 yard of 45-inch-wide terry cloth, in one color**
- **3/8 yard of 45-inch-wide terry cloth, in contrasting color**
- **1 piece of interfacing, 2x14-1/2''**
- **1 pair shoelaces, 18 inches long**

MAKING PONCHO

Enlarge the pattern, using the technique described on page 12. Cut out the pattern pieces according to the pattern shown in Figure A. Cut two sections from each piece of fabric.

Alternate placement of colored fabric. Stitch one section to the next, until you have stitched seven edges together. Sew 1/4-inch seams.

On the eighth edge, stitch 5-1/2 inches up from the bottom. Leave the rest of the seam unsewn as an opening. Stitch an intersecting line across the top of this seam to reinforce stitches at the opening.

Clip in the seam above the intersecting line on each side to make the open seam lie flat. On either side of the opening, hem raw edges to the wrong-side. Include ends of the shoelaces in the hem, 1/2 inch from the top edge.

Cut a bias strip of terry cloth 4x14-1/2'' for the collar. Cut interfacing the same size. Attach facing to the wrong-side of half of the collar. With right-sides together, fold the collar in half across the width and pin. Stitch 1/4-inch seams at the short ends. Turn right-side out. Center and pin the collar on the poncho, matching raw edges.

Stitch the outside of the collar to the neckline with 1/4-inch seams. On the inside, fold the raw edges of the collar under and hem with an invisible-hem-stitch.

Figure A—Poncho pattern. For the collar, cut a strip 4x14-1/2''.

Each square equals 1 inch.

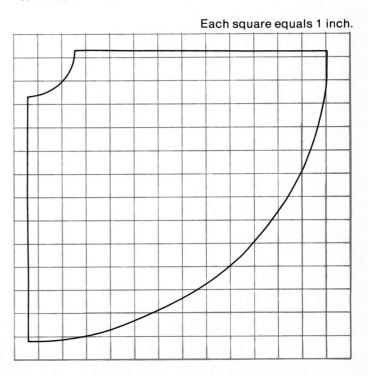

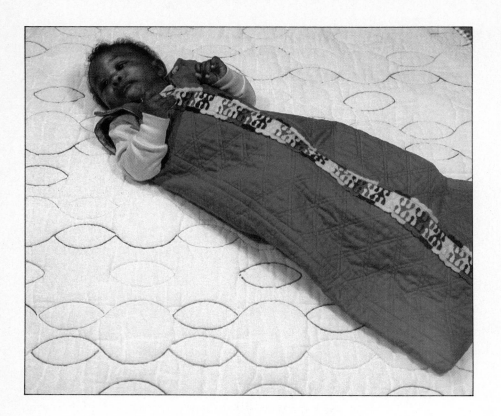

Sleeping Bag

In addition to providing warmth, a prequilted sleeping bag lets baby move and gives him room to grow.

EQUIPMENT
- Enlarging supplies, page 12
- Pattern-making supplies, page 15
- Sewing supplies

MATERIALS
- 1-1/8 yards of 45-inch-wide prequilted fabric
- 1-3/4 yards trim
- 4 yards grosgrain ribbon
- 6 snaps
- 4 small, decorative buttons

MAKING BAG

Preshrink fabric, page 16. Enlarge the pattern, using the technique described on page 12. Cut out the pattern pieces according to the pattern shown in Figure A. Place the sleeping-bag-back section on the fold of fabric, and cut it out. Cut two front pieces along the straight grain.

Take one front piece, right-side up, and fold the long edge under 1/4 inch. Stitch the edge. Trim will be added later to hide raw edges. Repeat this procedure for the other front piece. Fold the long edge under 1/4 inch and stitch. See Figure B.

Sew snaps 1/2 inch inside the edge on both pieces. Place them 4-1/2 inches apart. This keeps snaps out of the way of the sewing-machine needle when trim is added. Pin trim in position on both pieces. Stitch the trim along both sides.

Pin together the raw edges of the prequilted fabric. With right-sides together, stitch the front pieces to the back piece along the side and bottom seam of the bag. Finish with zigzag- or double-stitching.

To make the bag reversible, raw edges must be finished. Bind the bottom side of the bag with ribbon or bias tape around the neck, straps, armholes, sides and bottom. As indicated on the pattern, add buttonholes and buttons at shoulder edges. See page 7 for information on buttonholes.

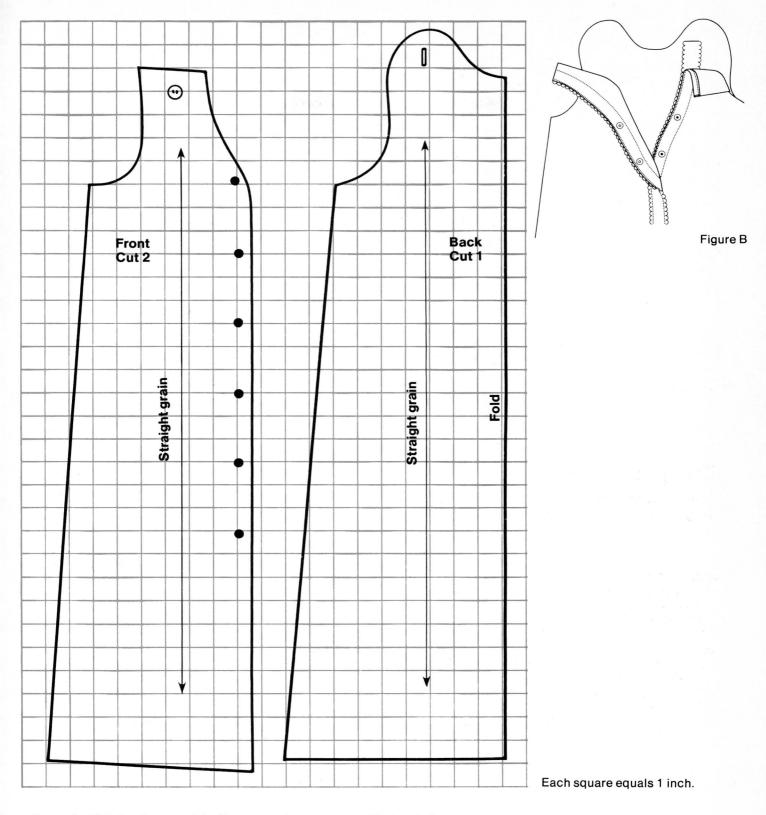

Front
Cut 2

Straight grain

Back
Cut 1

Straight grain

Fold

Figure B

Each square equals 1 inch.

Figure A—This bag is reversible. You can make yours one-sided and eliminate one set of buttons and half the trim.

One-Piece Sunsuit

This one-piece sunsuit is made from a simple pattern and stretch fabric. It lets baby move around in cool comfort.

EQUIPMENT
- Enlarging supplies, page 12
- Sewing supplies

MATERIALS
For a sunsuit fitting a child up to 18 pounds:
- 1/4 yard terry or other stretch fabric, any width
- 1/8 yard cotton or broadcloth for facing, any width
- 3 sets of 1/2-inch snaps
- 5 inches of Velcro
- 1 piece of elastic, 12 inches long
- 1 iron-on appliqué, optional

MAKING SUNSUIT

Enlarge the pattern, using the technique described on page 12. Cut out the pattern pieces according to the pattern shown in Figure A.

Sew two strap pieces together along both long sides and across one end. Clip corners and turn. Repeat for the other strap. On the back piece, attach straps and lining to the fabric at the same time. See Figure B. Place right-sides together, with the straps inside.

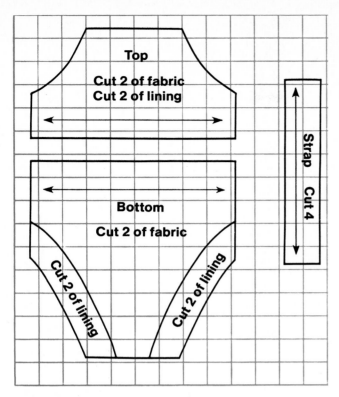

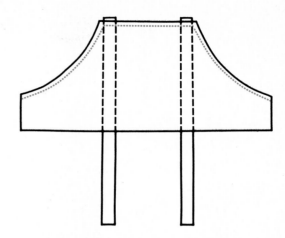

Figure B—Sew raw edges of straps in seam.

Figure A—When laying pattern pieces on stretch fabric, make sure fabric stretches in direction of arrows.

Each square equals 1 inch.

With right-sides together, sew the lining and front top together. Sew lining along the leg holes on all four pieces with a 1/4-inch seam. Turn to the wrong-side. On the leg holes of the front piece, fold the raw edges under 1/4 inch and press. Fold under 1/4 inch again, press and machine- or hand-stitch. On the leg holes of the back piece, add a narrow strip of elastic, page 9.

Sew the top pieces to the bottom pieces. Attach the appliqué any place you desire. Sew the pile side of the Velcro snap to the top of the inside front. See Figure C. Sew the hook side to the ends of each strap. Velcro keeps the straps attached over the shoulder. Pin and sew side seams together.

To finish the crotch opening, fold the open edge toward the facing. Fold under raw edges. Pin and sew the bottom snaps in position on the back piece. Pin and sew the top snaps on the front piece. See Figure C.

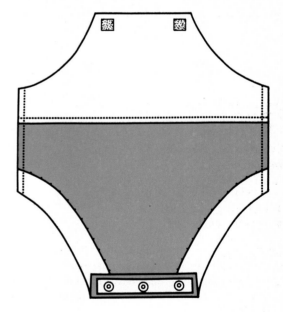

Figure C

Two-Piece Sunsuit

Like the one-piece sunsuit, the two-piece set is made from stretch fabric. The 1/3 yard of fabric needed for the width will leave enough scraps for a second pair of shorts or a top.

EQUIPMENT
- **Enlarging supplies, page 12**
- **Sewing supplies**

MATERIALS
For a sunsuit fitting a child up to 13 pounds:
- **1/3 yard of 60-inch-wide stretch fabric**
- **1/2 yard of 1/2-inch-wide elastic**
- **2 yards stretchy seam binding**

MAKING TOP
Enlarge the pattern, using the technique described on page 12. Cut out the pattern pieces according to the pattern shown in Figure A. Beginning with the straps, sew binding along one long edge of each strap. See page 6 for adding binding. Binding becomes the inside-neck edge, not part of the armhole.

Next work on the front and back pieces. Sew binding across both neck pieces on the right-side only. Binding on the wrong-side is left open to join the straps.

To add straps, begin with one of the front pieces. Move the stitched side of the bias on the neck back away from the raw edges. Put wrong-sides together, and match raw edges of the neck and strap. Pin and stitch straps. Finish the neck by pulling binding over all raw edges and stitching lines. Stitch across. See Figure B. In the same way, attach the loose ends of the straps to the second front piece.

For armholes, trim excess binding from the neck to match pattern shape. Add binding to the armholes. See Figure C.

With right-sides together, baste the front piece to the back piece along the side edges. Stitch together and turn right-side out and hem. See page 13 for hemming-stitches.

MAKING PANTS
With right-sides together, stitch the two pants pieces on each side along the seam lines. Arrange the sewn sections so the seam is in the middle, extending from the crotch to the waist on either side.

At the waist, make a casing for the elastic, page 9, and add the elastic. Hem the open portion of casing. Next add binding to the leg holes. With right-sides together, stitch the crotch closed.

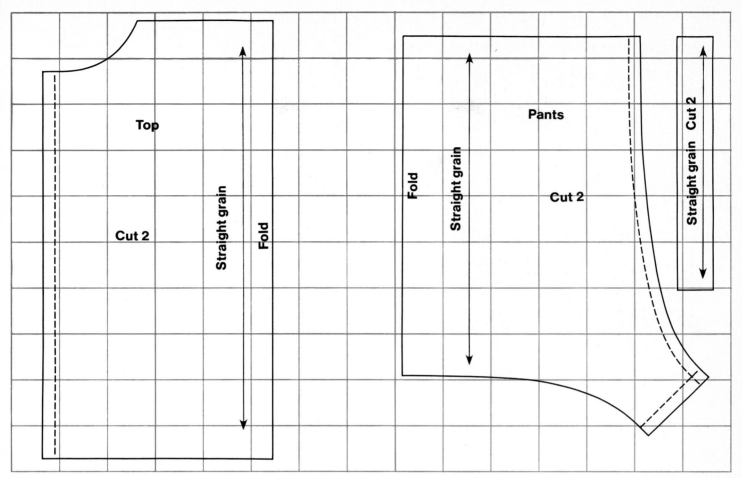

Figure A

Each square equals 1 inch.

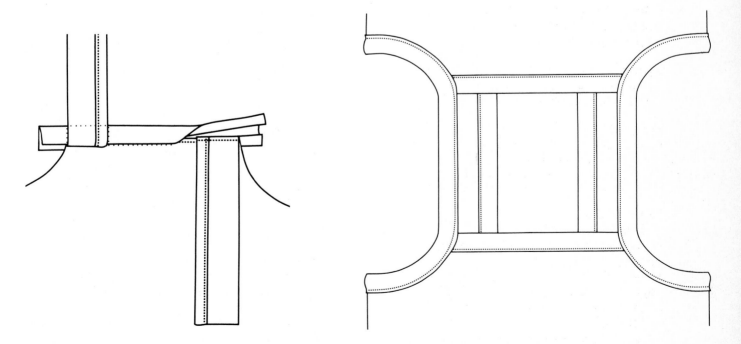

Figure B—When binding is stitched, lift each strap and hand-stitch to binding on both edges.

Figure C—See page 6 for more on adding binding to curved areas.

Nightie

Baby will stay comfortable in this soft sleepwear. The nightie can also be dressed-up with added trim.

EQUIPMENT
Sewing supplies

MATERIALS
For a nightie fitting a baby up to 15 pounds:
- 1-5/8 yard of 45-inch-wide velour, flannel or other soft fabric
- 1/2 yard of wide bias tape
- Trim. Amounts will vary, but a nightie this size measures 22 inches from the neckline to the hem edge.
- 3 sets of mediumweight Velcro snaps

MAKING NIGHTIE
Enlarge the pattern, using the technique described on page 12. Cut out the pattern pieces according to the pattern shown in Figure A. Lay paper pattern pieces on the fabric. Both front and back pieces are laid along the fold.

On the front piece, cut open the center for the front opening. Baste, then stitch, each sleeve to the front and back at the shoulder seams, with right-sides together. Seams are 1/4 inch.

Pin and stitch the front piece to the back piece, with right-sides together. Machine-stitch side and underarm seams. Clip corners before turning right-side out. See Figure B.

Baste and sew trim to the front. Attach it from raw edge to raw edge. See Figure C for the *Kimono Jacket,* page 69. On each side of the front opening, finish raw edges by turning the facing to the wrong-side, then stitching in place. Before finishing raw edges, fold over the edges of the front. Determine placement of the Velcro snaps on the facing, and stitch in position. Stitching on the snaps will not show on the right-side.

To finish raw edges on the front opening, press raw edges to the wrong-side of the fabric. Use a 1/4-inch seam allowance. Fold the raw edges under 1/4 inch and press. Fold under 1/4 inch again, press and machine- or hand-stitch.

Finish the neck edge with bias tape, page 6. Leave a 1/4-inch piece of extra bias on each end for mitering corners to the wrong-side of the fabric, page 14. Hem sleeves and bottom edges.

Fold

Straight grain

Straight grain

Fold

Back

Front

Each square equals 1 inch.

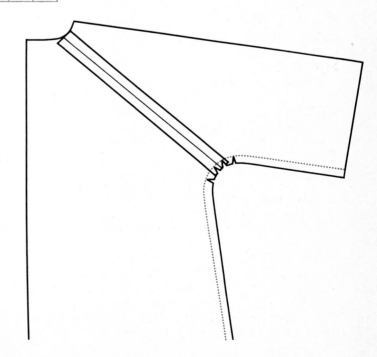

Figure B—Sew sleeve in position on both sides at shoulder before joining side and underarm seams.

Pinafore and toddler sunbonnet. The toddler sunbonnet pattern is found on page 78.

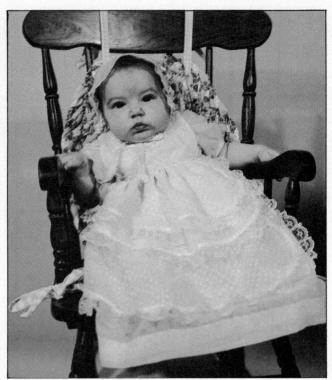

Christening pinafore.

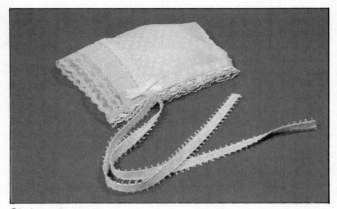

Christening hat.

Pinafore

This is an easy-to-make pinafore with open sides. It can be a cool sundress or a finishing touch to a fancy outfit. This project will fit a small baby or a toddler. Patterns for dresses are not included, but similar types are sold by pattern companies. Instructions for Sunbonnet can be found on page 78. See page 67 for the Christening Hat.

EQUIPMENT

- Enlarging supplies, page 12
- Sewing supplies
- Stuffing tool to turn small corners, page 18

MATERIALS

- 1/2 yard of 45-inch-wide fabric for the two-layered skirt
- 3 yards trim
- 1-1/2 yards ribbon for waist, in any width
- 6-strand embroidery floss, for belt loops
- 1 hook and eye

64

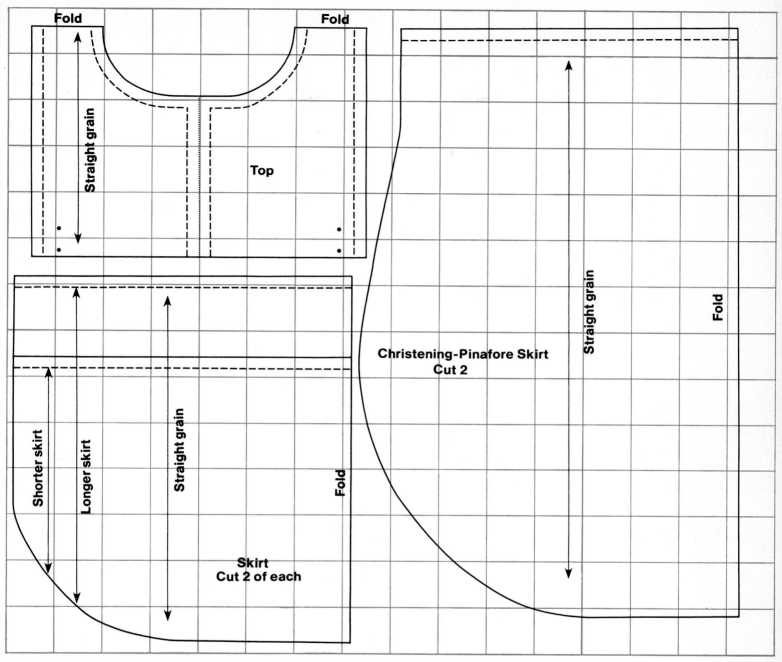

Figure A

Fold

Fold

Straight grain

Top

Straight grain

Fold

Christening-Pinafore Skirt
Cut 2

Shorter skirt

Longer skirt

Straight grain

Fold

Skirt
Cut 2 of each

Each square equals 1 inch.

MAKING TOP

Enlarge the pattern, using the technique described on page 12. Cut out the pattern pieces as shown in the pattern shown in Figure A. Cut two top pieces on the fold as shown in the pattern. Open both pieces and cut the back openings. With right-sides together, sew 1/4-inch seams along both sides and around back and neck opening. See Figure B on page 66.

If you want to include a ruffle or lace trim along the outside edges, sew trim in seams at this point. See page 17 for adding ruffles.

Turn the pinafore right-side out. For corners at the top of the back opening, gently push the fabric out with a chopstick or other stuffing tool. If desired, add lace or trim at the neckline. Sew a hook and eye to the back opening now or when the pinafore is finished.

MAKING LAYERED SKIRT

Enlarge the pattern, using the technique described on page 12. Cut out the pattern pieces according to the pattern shown in Figure A. Cut four pieces of the pinafore skirt.

Before sewing the layers together, add trim or hem the bottom raw edges for the front and back skirts of the pinafore. Turn the raw edges to the wrong-side of the fabric if you are hemming without trim. If you include trim, turn raw edges to the right-side of the fabric. Sew the trim on top of the turned edges.

Match the raw edges of both waist pieces. Layer the skirts for the front and back. Gather the waist to the measurement of the width of the bodice piece. See page 12 for gathering.

Baste and sew skirts to the top piece at the waist. Use a 1/4-inch seam. Sew together with right-sides facing and raw edges matching.

BRAIDING BELT LOOPS

Thread a six-strand piece of embroidery floss on a needle. Knot one end. With the knot on the wrong-side of the waist, bring the needle through to the right-side of fabric at the waistline. Remove the needle.

Divide the six strands into three sets of two strands each and braid. See page 7 for braiding. The length of the braid depends on the width of the ribbon you use for the belt. Leave enough room so the ribbon can easily slide through the loops but not so much that the ribbon slides up and down at the waist.

When braiding is complete, thread the needle again with all six strands. Push the needle through the bodice piece at the desired position. Knot the thread on the wrong-side of the fabric. Repeat for remaining four loops. See markings on Figure B for positioning loops.

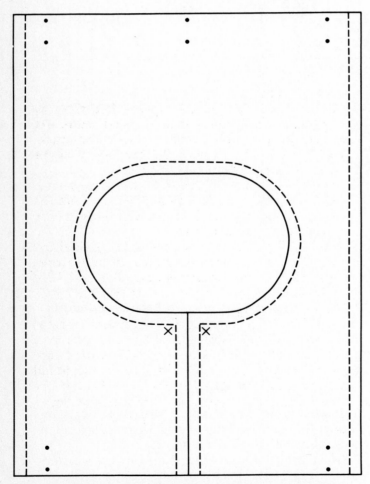

Figure B—Dots indicate belt loop placement. X's are for hook and eye.

Christening Pinafore and Hat

Five yards of trim and 1 yard of fabric are needed for the christening pinafore. Enough fabric will be left to make a christening hat. The skirt for this version has three layers, instead of two. For the additional pattern piece, see Figure A. Before cutting the fabric, be sure the pattern for the pinafore matches the size of your christening-dress pattern. If the patterns do not fit, adjust the pinafore top to fit the dress.

EQUIPMENT
● **Sewing supplies**

MATERIALS
● **1 square of fabric, 11x11''**
● **1 piece of broad, unruffled lace, 11 inches long for rim**
● **1/3 yard of narrow, ruffled lace for the bottom edge**
● **2 or more tiny bows, optional**

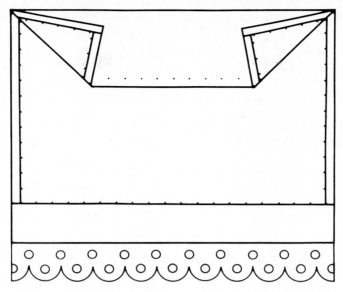

Figure C—The amount folded may vary, depending on the size of lace and baby's head.

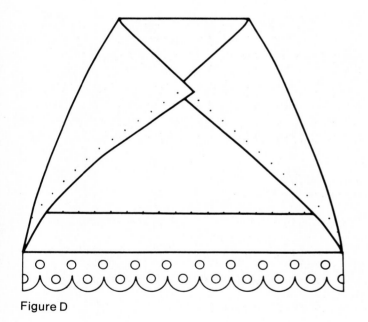

Figure D

MAKING HAT

On all four sides of the square, fold the raw edges under 1/4 inch and press. Fold under 1/4 inch again, press and machine- or hand-stitch. See Figure C. Turn under the raw edges of the wide lace at each short end and hem.

Turn the square of fabric to the wrong-side. Sew lace along one edge inside the hem. Fold the front edge so the lace is on the right-side of the square. Press and tack in place.

For the back of the hat, fold the edge about 2-1/2 inches to the wrong-side of the fabric. Press the fold and the corners. See Figure C. Fold the outside corners to the center. See Figure D. Tack the layers together at this center point.

Turn the hat inside out. Fold the extra fabric at the back in a neat triangle and tack in position. Turn the hat right-side out. Add ruffled lace around the bottom edges, then sew additional lace to the ribbon. Attach ribbon to the top of the hem on the right-side of the hat. If desired, finish with decorative bows. See photo on page 64.

Kimono robe in prequilted fabric.

Kimono jacket and booties. Booties pattern and instructions are found on page 73.

Kimono vests.

Kimono robe in panne velvet.

Kimono Jacket, Robe and Vest

Made from only one pattern piece, here is a simple jacket that can be made reversible, with a sleeve in two styles. For variations of this pattern, see the Robe version, page 70, and the Vest version, page 72.

EQUIPMENT
- **Enlarging supplies, page 12**
- **Sewing supplies**

MATERIALS
For jacket fitting child up to 25 pounds:
- **1 piece of prequilted, two-sided fabric, 23x27″**
- **3 yards of double-fold bias binding for straight sleeve**
- **5 yards of double-fold bias binding for box-cut sleeve**
- **2 yards ribbon, rickrack, braid or other trim. If you do not want to make your jacket reversible, only 1-1/3 yards is needed.**
- **2/3 yard of 1/2-inch-wide grosgrain ribbon for side seams, optional**

MAKING PATTERN

Before making patterns, measure your child. Adjust pattern length, if necessary. Fold the paper for the pattern in quarters and draw squares. Enlarge the pattern, using the technique described on page 12. Cut out the pattern piece according to the pattern shown in Figure A. Unfold and mark the front-neckline curves. Cut down the center fold mark for front only.

MAKING JACKET

Lay the paper pattern on the fabric. Pin the pattern in place and cut around the cutting lines. Remove the pattern piece.

Baste double-fold bias seam binding to sleeve edges. For the straight sleeve, end stitching 1/2 inch from the edge. See Figure B. Sleeve bias will be finished later. For the box sleeve, see Figure C. To find the amount of bias needed for box sleeves, measure around the sleeve and add 1 inch. This allows enough extra bias so raw edges can be turned under.

Ties for opening and closing the jacket are added at the same time as the trim. Set the ties under the ribbon about 1 inch from the neck. See Figures B and C. Reinforce ties with a second row of stitches. Baste and sew trim down the front.

Measure the amount of seam binding needed to finish the neckline, both sides and the bottom edge. Add a few extra inches so binding edges can be folded under. Fold the length of seam binding in half to determine the center. Pin the

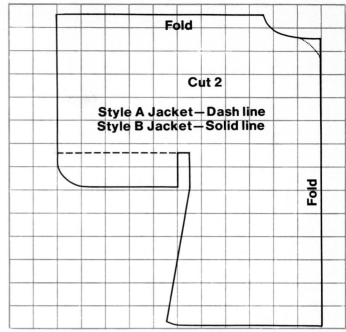

Each square equals 1 inch.

Figure A—Box-cut sleeve is marked in solid lines. Straight sleeve is indicated with dashes.

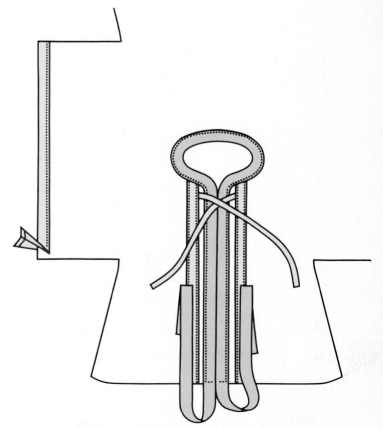

Figure B—Do not stitch last inch of binding to fabric on one side of each sleeve edge. Wait until seams are attached and finished. Trim, ties and binding are also sewn in place.

center of the seam binding to the center back of the neck. Baste seam binding around the neckline and down the front. Ease where necessary to fit curves.

Machine-stitch binding in place. Pin extra seam binding for the hemline out of the way of the side seams until you are ready to work on it. See Figure B.

Turn the jacket inside out. If you are making it reversible, you can sew on either side. Sew side seams, using the edge of the pressure foot to make a 1/2-inch seam allowance. Clip inside corners for easy turning. Do not clip corners if you plan to use seam allowances to finish the raw edges.

The seam allowance can be finished in two ways. Both ways are reversible. With the first method, use bias tape or grosgrain ribbon. Sew the tape or ribbon 1/16 inch from the side seam. See Figure D. Trim the seam allowance to 1/8 inch. Hand-stitch the other edge of the seam binding or ribbon to the garment to cover the trimmed seam allowance.

The second method to finish seams is to fold one layer of the seam allowance over the other part. Trim one layer of fabric and batting in the seam allowance to 1/8 inch. Leave one seam allowance 1/2 inch wide. Fold the seam allowance over the narrower seam allowance, and hand-stitch in place. See Figure E. Use a hem- or overcast-stitch. See pages 11 and 13 for stitches. Cover the trimmed seam allowance.

Miter corners on the bottom front. See page 14 for mitering and page 6 for binding. Using the remaining attached seam binding, baste and sew binding to the hem. See Figure F.

To finish the sleeves, join bias tape to the bottom of the sleeve. Use the same method as you used for the hem. To finish box-cut sleeves, lay the jacket right-side up. Sew bias trim on the sleeve from the armhole around the edge. See Figure F.

Robe *(See photo page 68.)*

The robe can be made with straight or box-cut sleeves. It is made the same way as the jacket, with some exceptions.

EQUIPMENT
- Enlarging supplies, page 12
- Sewing supplies

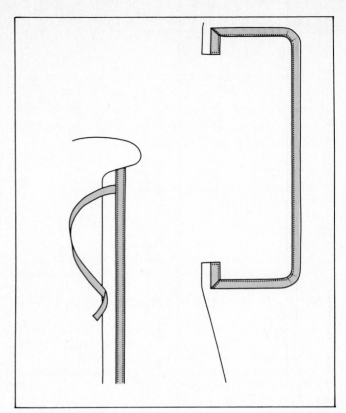

Figure C—Fold edges of bias over so raw edges do not show. If attaching bias by hand, use overcasting, page 11, or hem-stitch, page 13.

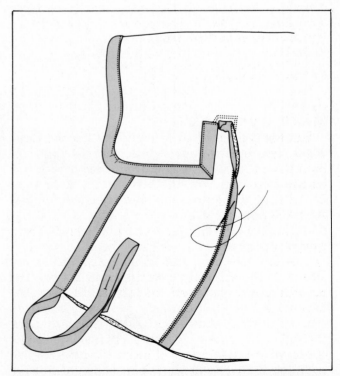

Figure D—Fold under raw edges of bias or ribbon before joining edges to sleeve binding.

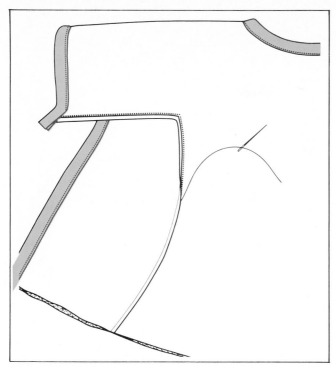

Figure E—For uncut seam allowance, choose widest side with least fraying.

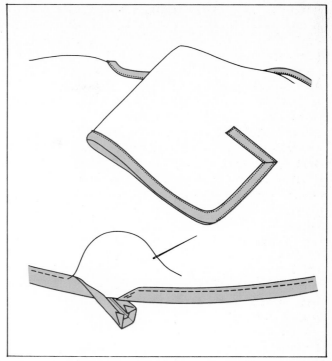

Figure F—Fold over edges so they close on center of back hem. Stitches finish bottom edge of box-cut sleeve.

MATERIALS

For a robe fitting a child up to 30 pounds:

- 1-1/2 yard panne velvet or prequilted fabric
- 1/4 yard fabric in contrasting color for binding and sash. This is unnecessary if you make the robe in prequilted fabric.
- 1 set of 2 mediumweight Velcro fasteners
- 1-1/3 yard bias tape or 1/2-inch-wide grosgrain ribbon for side seams, optional

MAKING PATTERN

Enlarge the pattern in Figure G using the technique described on page 69. Cut out the pattern pieces. Check Figure A for clarification of the pattern piece.

ADDING SEAM BINDING

If you make the robe from prequilted fabric, follow the procedure for making the jacket. If you make the jacket from non-quilted fabric, leave off the binding around the bottom edge. See the photograph of the panne velvet robe, page 70.

Sew binding down the front on both sides. End stitching 1 inch from the edge. Fold the raw edges under 1/4 inch and press. Fold under 1/4 inch again, press and machine- or hand-stitch. Pin, press and machine-stitch. Turn the binding back to the right-side.

Measure the amount of binding needed for

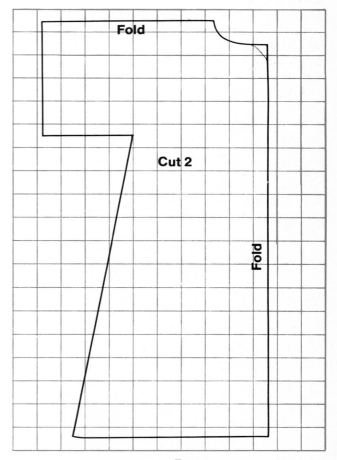

Each square equals 1 inch.

Figure G—Pattern for robe.

mitering corners. See page 14 for information on mitering. Add 1/4 inch for folding raw edges to the wrong-side before basting and stitching corners.

ADDING SASH

Measure two strips of fabric 2-1/4 inches wide, long enough to go around the child's waist and tie. If necessary, add iron-on interfacing to the wrong-side of one or both strips before pinning them together. Place right-sides together, and stitch a 1/4-inch seam down each side. Sew the bottom edge in a point or sew straight across, from side to side. Leave one end open.

Clip the corner and turn the robe right-side out. Along the lower edge, fold the raw edges under 1/4 inch and press. Fold under 1/4 inch again, press and machine- or hand-stitch.

To attach the sash, find the midpoint of the sash. Stitch the sash to the back of the robe. See Figure H.

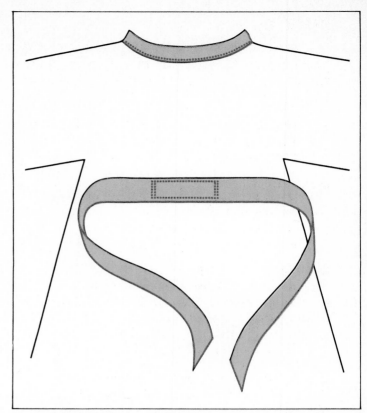

Figure H—Sew sash on robe. Reinforce sides with double stitches.

Vest *(See photo page 68.)*

The vest is a tapered version of the jacket. The garments are made the same way, with some exceptions.

EQUIPMENT
- Enlarging supplies, page 12
- Sewing supplies

MATERIALS
For a vest fitting a child up to 18 pounds:
- 2/3 yard of 45-inch-wide fabric. If using pre-quilted fabric, a 15x20'' piece is suitable.
- 2 yards of wide bias tape
- 1/2 yard trim
- 1/4 yard bias tape or 1/2-inch-wide grosgrain ribbon for side seams, optional

For a vest fitting a child up 25 pounds:
- 3/4 yard of 45-inch-wide fabric. If using pre-quilted fabric, a 18x26'' piece is suitable.
- 3 yards of wide bias tape
- 2/3 yard of decorative trim
- 1 yard of ribbon for tie
- 1/3 yard bias tape or grosgrain ribbon for side seams, optional

MAKING PATTERN

Enlarge the pattern in Figure A, using the technique described on page 69. Cut out the pattern piece according to the pattern shown in Figure I.

ADDING SEAM BINDING

Begin by basting and sewing the binding around the armholes. To find the amount of binding needed for the armholes, measure the

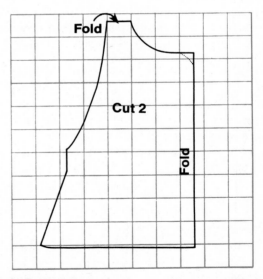

Figure I—Pattern for vest.   Each square equals 1 inch.

armhole and add 1 inch. This allows extra bias so the edges will overlap. See the way the binding is added to the sleeves in Figure B. Sew the side seams. Finish edges of binding on the armhole by overlapping and stitching.

Booties

These booties are shown on page 68 with the Kimono Jacket. Booties tie at the ankle and are almost impossible to kick off. They are prequilted and snugly.

EQUIPMENT
- **Enlarging supplies, page 12**
- **Sewing supplies**

MATERIALS
- **1/4 yard of 45-inch-wide prequilted fabric**
- **1/3 yard of single-fold binding**
- **1 pair of shoelaces, 18 inches long**
- **12 craft pompons, optional**

MAKING PATTERN

Enlarge the pattern, using the technique described on page 12. Cut out the pattern pieces according to the pattern shown in Figure A. The pattern in Figure A will fit a baby with a size-3 foot. If making another size, trace the bottom of a shoe in the correct sole size. Add 1 inch in length for a seam allowance and growth.

Use the grid system as a guide. Enlarge or reduce the pattern for the rest of the bootie to fit the sole piece you have made.

SEWING BOOTIES

Attach seam binding around the cuff area between points A and C. Extend binding 1/2 inch beyond the seam line on each side. See page 6 for adding binding. Repeat for the opposite side of the bootie. Make hand- or machine-stitched buttonholes at points noted on the pattern. See page 7 for buttonholes.

With right-sides together, sew from Point A to Point B with a 1/4-inch seam. Stitch the top seam line from Point C to Point D. With right-sides together, pin the completed top piece to the bottom of the shoe. Begin with the heel, then sew the toe. Finish with the sides. Baste and machine- or whip-stitch with a 1/4-inch seam. See page 14 for whip-stitch. If adding a face, stitch pompons by hand through all three layers of quilted fabric. Use the photograph as a guide or design your own. If desired, add eye buttons to the pompons. These buttons can be found in craft-supply stores. To finish, weave shoelaces through buttonholes.

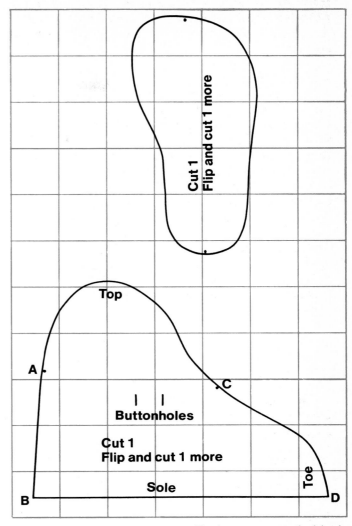

Each square equals 1 inch.

Figure A—When marking the fabric, flip pattern pieces as indicated.

Party Dress

This project is for the more-experienced seamstress. It is a special-occasion dress with ruffles, flounces and an organdy petticoat.

EQUIPMENT
- **Enlarging supplies, page 12**
- **Sewing supplies**

MATERIALS
For a baby up to 16 pounds:
- **1-1/2 yards of 60-inch-wide panne velvet or other stretch fabric**
- **1 piece of organdy, 5-1/2x66''**
- **2 pieces fusible interfacing, 1-1/2x7-1/2''**
- **Kit to cover 4 buttons or snaps, optional**

MAKING PATTERN
Enlarge the pattern for the bodice pieces, using the technique described on page 12. Cut out the pattern pieces according to the pattern shown in Figure A. If your fabric has a nap, each piece for the dress must be cut in the same direction.

The skirt is made from strips sewn in tiers. The top and middle tiers are 3-1/8x66''. For the bottom tier, three 2-1/4x33'' pieces are sewn together to make a piece 99 inches in length. If your fabric is not 66 inches wide, sew smaller strips together to make a 66-inch length.

To make this tiered skirt on a purchased dress pattern, follow these steps. First, determine the length needed for the two upper strips. Do this by measuring the bodice waist. Multiply this measurement by three. On the dress in this pattern, the waist is 22 inches: 22 x 3 = 66 inches.

To determine the length needed for the lower strip, add 50% more to the tripled measurement: 66 + 33 = 99 inches. To find the length needed for each section of the lower strip, divide the total by three. For this size, cut three strips 33 inches long.

The width of the strips varies according to size. The top two tiers are the same width. The bottom tier is wider. If the length from the waist to the hem is 7 inches, 25% of this figure is 1-3/4 inches. Add 1/2 inch to this for seam allowances. The width needed for the bottom tier is 2-1/4 inches. To find the width for the top and middle tiers, divide the remaining 75% by two. Add 1/2 inch to each measurement for seam allowances. For a 7-inch length, the width for each upper tier is 2-5/8 inches, plus 1/2-inch seam allowances. This totals 3-1/8 inches.

MAKING BODICE
With right-sides together, sew the bodice pieces at the shoulder. For the back opening, fold the raw edges under 1/4 inch along each side to the wrong-side of fabric. Press. Fold under 1-1/2 inches and press again. These fold lines are marked on back-bodice piece. Cut out interfacing for the back opening. If you are making another size, the width is still 1-1/2 inches. The length depends on the length of the back piece. Add facing to the back opening and press.

For the ruffle at the neck, cut a strip of fabric 2 inches wide and twice as long as the neck measurement, plus 1/2 inch for a seam allowance. Fold in half and press lengthwise. Sew edges together, then make the ruffle by hand or machine. See page 17.

For bias at the neck, cut a piece of fabric the length of the neck, plus seam allowances. Cut fabric 5/8 inch wide. Turn the raw edges of all four sides under 1/8 inch to the wrong-side of the fabric and press.

With right-sides together and raw edges matching, pin the ruffle to the neck. Fold the extra length at the ends toward the inside of the ruffle. Baste the edge of the binding along the same seam. The right-side of the binding faces the ruffle. Machine-stitch and turn binding to cover the raw edges of the ruffle. Hem the loose edge of the binding to the neck. See Figure B.

ADDING SLEEVES
The casing and ruffle are added later when side and underarm seams are joined. Gather the top of the sleeve with a running-stitch between dots, page 11. Make a row of stitches along the fitting line and another row 1/4 inch above it. See Figure C. See page 12 for gathering.

Draw threads up to fit sleeve notches to arm-

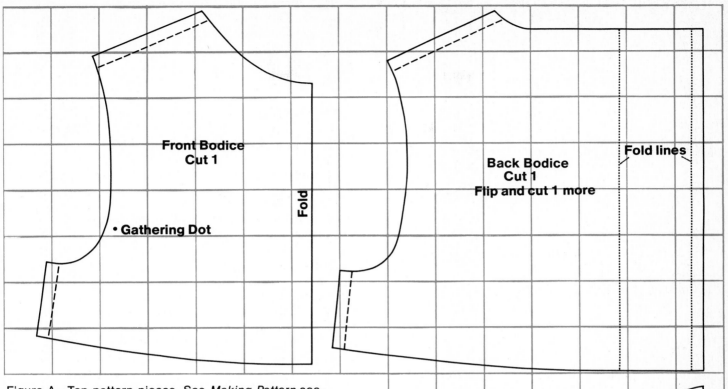

Figure A—Top pattern pieces. See *Making Pattern* section for dimensions and strips needed for skirt.

Front Bodice Cut 1

• Gathering Dot

Fold

Back Bodice Cut 1 Flip and cut 1 more

Fold lines

Sleeve Cut 2

• Gathering Dot

Fold

Each square equals 1 inch.

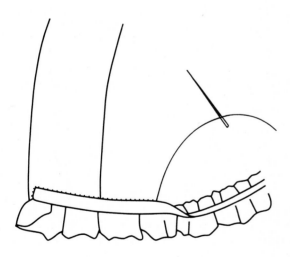

Figure B—Sew neck bias over raw edges of ruffle.

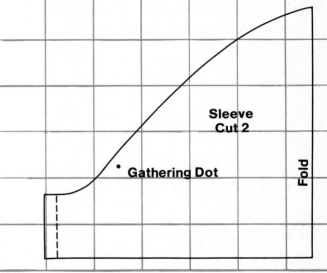

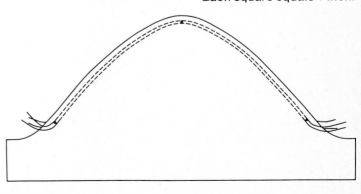

hole notches. Match the center mark at the top of the sleeve to the center of the shoulder seam. Pin the armhole and sleeve together. Hold the gathered top in a curve, wrong-side up. Tack along the lower gathering thread to evenly flatten fullness. Back-stitch to hold it firmly.

Machine-stitch below and above the fitting line. Press seams to one side or press open. Clip into seam allowances.

Figure C—Gather sleeve top with two lines of running-stitches.

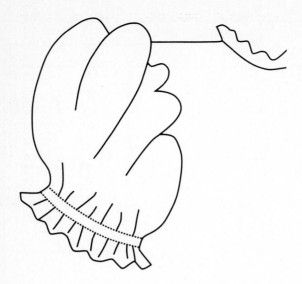

Figure D—Add casing for elastic.

STITCHING SIDE AND UNDERARM SEAMS

Make two ties for the sash, each 22-1/2 inches long. See page 18. With right-sides together, pin the front and back pieces at the sides. Place the ends of the ties between the seams. Stitch the side and underarm seams in one continuous seam. Press seams open.

FINISHING SLEEVES

On each sleeve, fold the raw edges under 1/4 inch and press. Fold under another 2 inches, press and machine-stitch the hem to the inside of the sleeve. Leave a 1-inch opening for elastic. Machine-stitch a second row to form a casing 5/8 inch from this stitching.

Cut a piece of 1/2-inch elastic 1/2 inch larger than the measurement around the child's upper arm. Draw the elastic through the casing. See page 9 for adding elastic. Lap ends and sew together by hand. Hem the opening closed.

MAKING SKIRT AND PETTICOAT

Skirt—Beginning with the top tier, stitch together the ends of the 66-inch strip. Press seams open. Gather the upper edge to fit the bodice waist, page 12.

On the second tier, stitch together the short ends of the 66-inch strip. Press seams open. Gather the upper edge of the middle tier. With right-sides together, pin the upper edge of the middle tier to the lower edge of the upper tier. Adjust gathers and stitch. Press seams open.

For the lower tier, stitch sections together at the ends. Press the seams open. Hem the lower tier before sewing it to the middle tier. Fold the raw edges under 1/4 inch and press. Fold under 1/4 inch again, press and machine- or hand-stitch.

Gather the upper edge of the lower tier. With right-sides together, pin the upper edge of the lower tier to the lower edge of the middle tier. Adjust gathers and stitch. See Figure E. Press seams open.

Petticoat—Hem the bottom edge of the organdy before gathering. Fold the raw edges under 1/4 inch and press. Fold under 1/4 inch again, press and machine- or hand-stitch. Gather the top edge, page 12. Match the raw edges of the organdy and velvet, and baste them together. With right-sides together, pin and baste the bodice to the skirt pieces, with the seam allowance about 3/4 inch longer on the top. Stitch together.

To protect baby's stomach from the rough organdy, pull the raw edges of the top up over the waist. *Baste* organdy in place. This makes the organdy easy to remove for machine washing. Organdy adds bounce to the skirt, but it is not comfortable to wear. After the party is over or the photograph taken, you may decide not to use the petticoat.

Add snaps or buttons to the back opening at regular intervals. You can use snaps on the inside as a closure with decorative buttons on the outside.

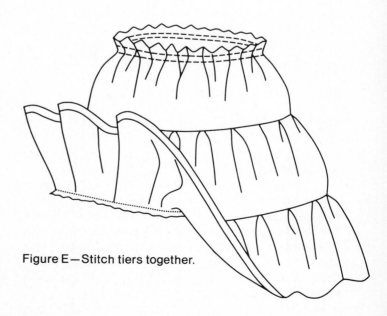

Figure E—Stitch tiers together.

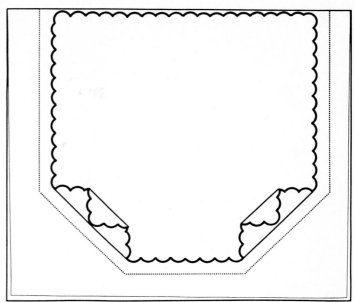

Figure A—Mark 1/2-inch seam allowance with pen before cutting. Make seam width of plastic the same all the way around. Trim only top inside layer of plastic.

Handkerchief Bib

This bib can be made from a man's or woman's handkerchief. Covering it with plastic makes fancy lacework or linen a practical bib.

EQUIPMENT
- **Sewing or embroidery supplies**

MATERIALS
- **1/2 yard mediumweight, clear plastic, in any width**
- **1 handkerchief, in any size**
- **1 yard 1/2-inch-wide grosgrain ribbon**

MAKING BIB

Fold down the two top corners of the handkerchief and bring the tips back up. See Figure A. Press. Handkerchiefs vary in size, so the amount that is folded varies. The neck opening needs to be at least 5 inches across.

Measure a piece of plastic twice as long as the handkerchief. Fold the plastic in half. Slip the handkerchief between the plastic layers with the bottom end on the fold. See Figure A.

Set the iron on the lowest setting. Place a damp towel between the bib and plastic. Do not place the iron directly on the plastic. Press. Plastic will smooth out and soften, securing the handkerchief in plastic.

Cut the three sides not on the fold 1/2 inch larger than the handkerchief. See the dotted line in Figure A.

Fold over the raw edges 1/4 inch along a long side. Press. Fold another 1/4 inch and press again.

Follow the same steps for the other long edge, pressing plastic under to the same side. Press edges where the handkerchief has been folded. Before folding neck edges, trim the bulk from each corner. Fold the last raw edge under 1/4

inch. Press. Fold and press again as with the other side.

Slip one end of the ribbon under the plastic at the corner. Machine-stitch in position. See Figure B. Repeat for the other side. Lift straps and tack in position.

FINISHING BIB

To finish the bib, sew the edges of the pressed seams. The type of stitch depends on the kind of handkerchief you use. An almost-invisible slip-stitch is good for patterned fabric. A plain handkerchief can be embroidered with a more decorative chain-stitch. See page 9 for stitches.

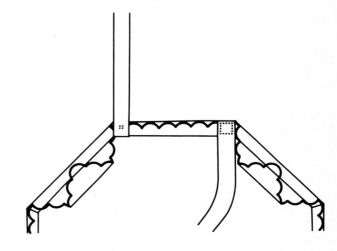

Figure B—Sew ribbon to plastic with square of stitches.

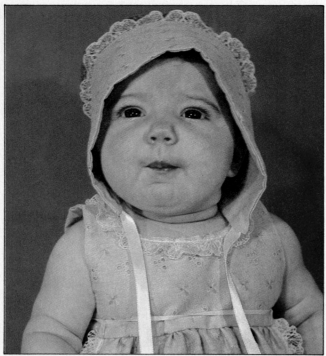

Infant sunbonnet. The toddler sunbonnet is shown on page 64.

Sunbonnet

This cute bonnet is easy to make by hand or machine. It can be tailored to fit an infant or toddler.

EQUIPMENT
- Enlarging supplies, page 12
- Sewing supplies

MATERIALS
- 3/8 yard of 45-inch-wide fabric
- 2/3 yard of lace for trim
- 2/3 yard of ribbon for ties
- 1 piece of elastic for back of hat, 7 inches long
- 1 piece of non-fusible interfacing for large hat brim, 10x18″

MAKING INFANT HAT FRONT

Enlarge the pattern, using the technique described on page 12. Cut out the pattern pieces according to the pattern shown in Figure A. Before enlarging the pattern, measure baby's head from ear to ear over the top of the head. This will help you find the correct length of the hat front. Cut fabric and interfacing according to the pattern.

MAKING HAT BACK

Make a casing along the bottom edge for elastic, as indicated on the pattern. See Figure A. Add elastic, page 9. With a 1/4-inch seam, gather the remaining edges of the back piece to fit the inside rim of the front piece. See page 12 for gathering. With right-sides together, pin the back piece to the brim along these gathered edges. Baste and stitch.

See the markings in Figure A for the places to attach ribbons. To add ribbon, fold the raw edges of one end to the wrong-side and press. Sew this end to the brim with top-stitching. Repeat for the other side.

MAKING BRIM

To make the infant-size brim, lay fabric on the fold before cutting it out. Interfacing is not needed. With wrong-sides together, iron the fold. Turn right-side out, and pin raw edges of the folded piece to the back piece. Add trim in the seam instead of along the outside edge.

TODDLER SUNBONNET

The hat described above will also fit a toddler. The back of the child's head is covered with the back piece of the hat. The brim extends beyond the face. See the photo of the girl on page 64.

The equipment and materials to make the hat for a toddler are the same as for an infant. Except for the brim construction, both sizes are made the same way.

Position interfacing on the wrong-side of one brim piece. Match raw edges along the straight edge. Carefully fold the seam allowance over the curved edge of the interfacing and press. Match the second brim piece to the first. Turn the curved edges of the second brim piece to the wrong-side of the fabric, so top and bottom brim pieces are the same size. Press.

Place the two brim pieces with wrong-sides together. Add trim, with raw edges sandwiched between the top and bottom brim pieces. Baste and top-stitch, page 12.

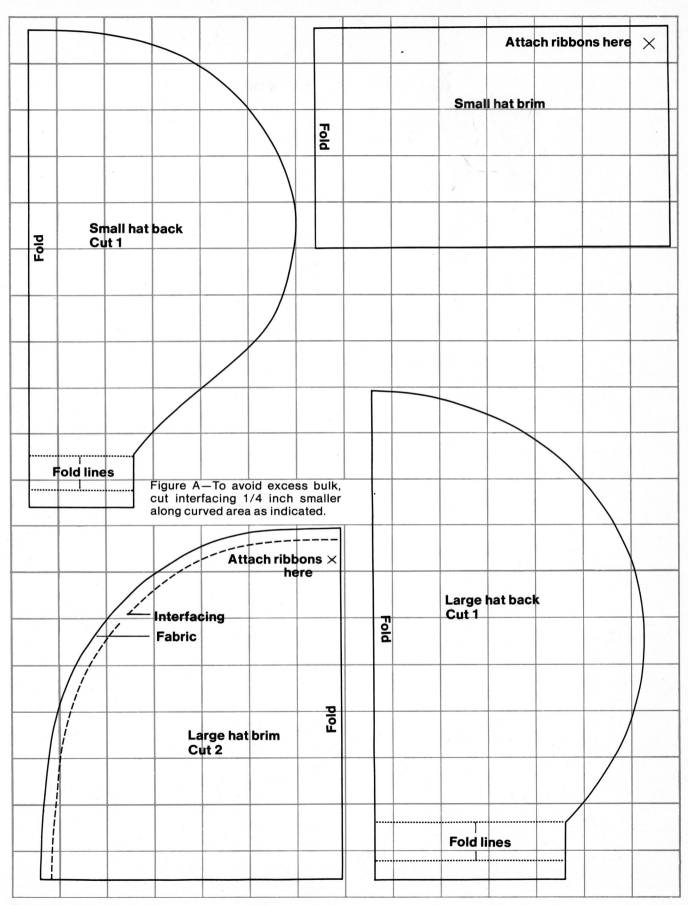

Attach ribbons here ✕

Small hat brim

Fold

**Small hat back
Cut 1**

Fold

Fold lines

Figure A—To avoid excess bulk, cut interfacing 1/4 inch smaller along curved area as indicated.

Attach ribbons ✕ **here**

Interfacing

Fabric

**Large hat back
Cut 1**

Fold

**Large hat brim
Cut 2**

Fold

Fold lines

Each square equals 1 inch.

Reversible Bib

With some prequilted fabric left from the Kimono Jacket, page 69, or other prequilted project, make this simple, dressy, reversible bib.

EQUIPMENT
- **Enlarging supplies, page 12**
- **Sewing supplies**

MATERIALS
- **1 piece of two-sided, prequilted fabric, 16x11″**
- **2 yards double-fold seam binding**
- **1 hook, snap or tie neck closure**
- **2/3 yard of trim, optional**

MAKING BIB

Enlarge the pattern, using the technique described on page 12. Cut out the pattern pieces according to the pattern shown in Figure A. Unfold the paper pattern, pin it on the fabric and cut it out.

Sew trim to the bib 1 inch inside the bottom edge. Find the midpoint of the double-fold seam binding and begin attaching the raw edges at the neck. To make the trough, turn up the bottom and sew the sides. Reinforce the stitches at the opening. By turning the trough to the other side, the bib becomes reversible.

Each square equals 1 inch.

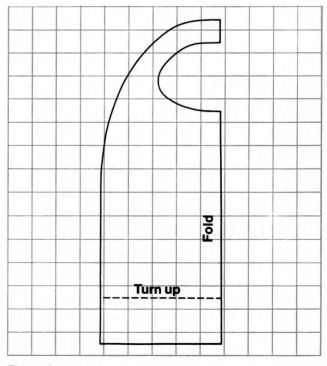

Figure A

Appliquéd Training Pants

When it's potty-training time, make the transition from diapers to training pants fun and rewarding. Personalize purchased training pants for your little girl or boy.

One quick, easy way to do this is with inexpensive, iron-on patches. Design a creature on paper or have an older child draw one. Cut the drawing in sections according to colors to be used for each part. Use these pieces as patterns when cutting the patches.

Follow package directions for the patches. Iron them in position on the training pants. To make sure the patches stay on in many washings, machine-stitch around the edge, as you would an appliqué. See Appliqués, page 5. The same idea can be used for T-shirts, as shown in the photograph.

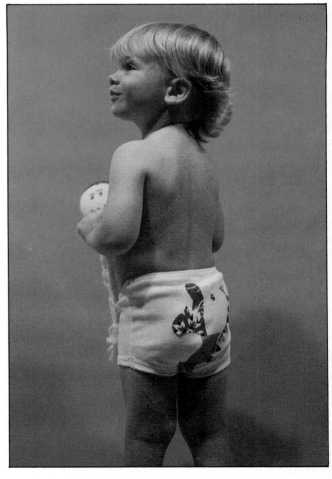

Stuffed Dolls and Toys

The stuffed toys in this section are easy to make. The *Octopus* and *Caterpillar*, page 84, do not even require sewing. Most of the projects are good for beginners because small amounts of material are needed. Babies won't criticize, so your efforts can be less-than-perfect and still be enjoyed by the recipient.

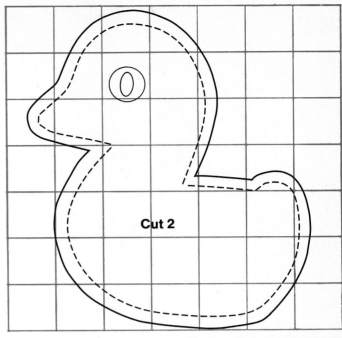

Each square equals 1 inch.

Figure A—Consider filling basket instead with a diaper pincushion for mom and dad, page 146.

Cut 2

Ducky in a Basket

Baby's first basket is filled with fun! You can use the ducky pattern shown here or trace another pattern from a cookie cutter.

EQUIPMENT

For the duck:
- **Enlarging supplies, page 12**
- **Transferring supplies, page 20**
- **Sewing supplies**
- **Stuffing tool, page 18**

For the basket:
- **Toothpick to apply glue**

MATERIALS

For the duck:
- **Less than 1/4 yard of 45-inch-wide soft, washable fabric, such as flannel**
- **Felt scraps for eyes**
- **Less than 1 bag of polyfill, page 18**

For the basket:
- **1 basket, with or without a handle, in any size. For a small basket, make 1 stuffed toy. For a large basket, make several toys.**
- **Ribbon and decorative trim. Amount depends on the size of the basket.**
- **White glue**

ENLARGING, TRANSFERRING, SEWING AND STUFFING

Enlarge the pattern, using the technique described on page 12. Cut out the pattern pieces according to the pattern shown in Figure A.

Duck's Eyes—Before stitching the duck pieces together, add the eyes. Felt does not require a seam allowance. Cut the eye and pupil from the patterns. See Figure A. With a small dot of white glue at the center of each circle, glue pieces to the duck's face. Glue does not permanently hold the eyes in place, but makes it easier for you to stitch the eyes in place.

You can also sew eyes with a satin-stitch, page 11, or other embroidery-stitch. See page 9 for information on different types of embroidery-stitches.

Left, Caterpillar. Above, Octopus.

Sock Toys

One pair of tube socks makes an octopus or two cuddly caterpillars. These washable, quickly made characters are stuffed and tied in parts. No sewing skills are needed, except for the optional hat to make for a doll or baby.

EQUIPMENT
For octopus or caterpillar:
- Scissors, page 20
- Permanent fabric markers, page 20

For the hat:
- Yarn needle, page 20
- 6-inch piece of 2x4'' cardboard for pompon
- Newspaper for work area

MATERIALS
For octopus or caterpillar:
- 1 pair tube socks, extra long
- 2 yards of yarn, strong thread or cord
- Less than 1 bag of polyfill, page 18

For the hat:
- 5 yards of rug yarn for pompon. Thinner yarn can be substituted, but the pompon will be floppy.

Or
- 1 premade pompon

GETTING READY
Wash and dry your socks before beginning the project. If making the octopus, cut the elastic top from each sock. Save them if you want to make a hat. Spread newspaper over your work area to catch sheddings.

STUFFING
Begin with one sock for either project. Pack the toe with the amount of stuffing desired for the head, page 18. If making the caterpillar, you are ready to tie the head of the toy in place with a double knot and bow. If making the octopus, pull the second sock snuggly over the first.

DECORATING
This toy is safe for baby because toxic ink fumes evaporate as it dries. However, a small child using these pens should be carefully supervised. Follow package directions.

Before decorating the face of either toy, practice with fabric markers on newspaper. The design you like best can be copied on the sock. If you prefer, draw the features on the sock with a tailor's tracing pen or pencil. If you make a mistake on the sock, include the mistake as part of the design.

FINISHING CATERPILLAR
Stuff and tie another ball under the first. Continue stuffing and tying balls. The number of parts your caterpillar has depends on the length of the sock and the amount of stuffing you use. Decorate the body with fabric markers.

FINISHING OCTOPUS
Fold the outside sock back over the head. This way you can cut one sock at a time. To cut the sock into strips for braiding, cut the inside sock in half lengthwise. Cut to within 1 inch of the head. Cut each half into half again, so you have four strips. To make 12 strips, cut each strip three more times. See Figure A.

Pull the outside sock back down. Cut it in 12 strips. Braid the strips into eight tentacles, page 7. When you get within 1 inch of the end, tie the braid securely with yarn or other material.

MAKE A HAT FOR A DOLL
Use leftover cuffs to make a hat for a doll or small infant. Cut each cuff section open along

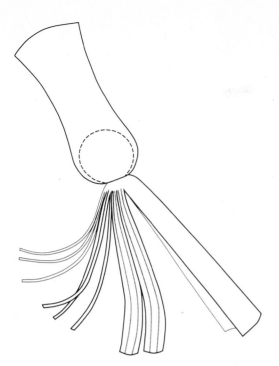

Figure A—When first sock is cut in strips, fold back outside. Cut outside in 12 strips.

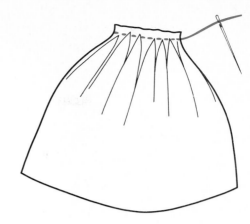

Figure B—To gather and close opening, pull yarn and knot securely.

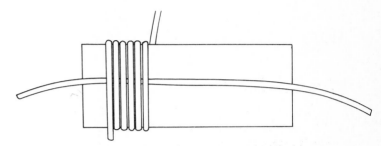

Figure C—When pompon is ready to be tied, you don't have to work another piece of yarn through loops.

Figure D—Join loops with secure knot, then clip ends.

one side. Thread the needle with a single ply of yarn. With right-sides facing, sew the cuffs together along each side. Use a 1/4-inch seam with small running-stitches. To gather and close the opening, pull the yarn and knot it securely. See Figure B. Turn the hat right-side out.

MAKING POMPON

Lay an 8-inch piece of yarn across the length of the cardboard. See Figure C. When the pompon is ready to be tied, this piece will already be through the loops. Wrap the cardboard with as much yarn as possible. Remove the cardboard and join the loops with a secure knot. See Figure D. Clip the ends of the loops.

ATTACHING POMPON

Position the pompon on top of the hat. Pull the two longer pieces of yarn through the hole. Keep the pompon in place as you turn the hat inside out. Thread the needle with one of the longer pieces. Make a running-stitch about halfway around, 1/4 inch under the first one.

Remove the needle, but don't knot the yarn. Thread the other strand and take a running-stitch around the other side. Remove the needle and tie the ends of each strand in a knot. See Figure E. Clip excess yarn.

Figure E

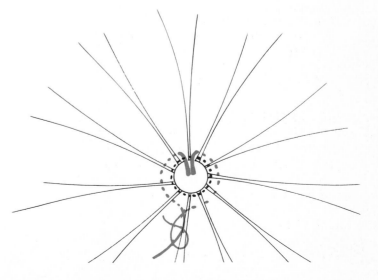

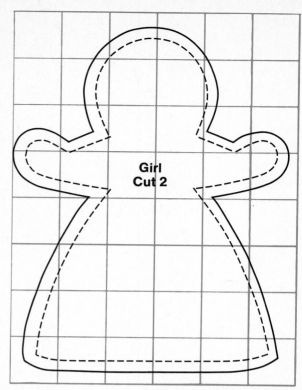

**Girl
Cut 2**

Figure A   Each square equals 1 inch.

Tiny Playmates

Look in your kitchen to find great ideas for making stuffed toys. These patterns, and ones in other projects, were traced from cookie cutters. Shapes can be enlarged to any size. These playmates range from 6 to 8 inches, a perfect size for baby's hands.

EQUIPMENT
- Enlarging supplies, page 12
- Sewing supplies
- Stuffing tool page 18
- Embroidery hoop, optional, page 21

MATERIALS
- Less than 1/3 yard of 45-inch-wide washable fabric
- 1 piece of fabric for skirt, 15x5''
- 5 inches of decorative ribbon
- 1/2 yard of eyelet trim for pinafore
- Thread to match fabric
- Small amount of embroidery thread for faces
- Less than 1 bag of polyfill, page 18

MAKING PATTERN
Enlarge the pattern, using the technique described on page 12. Cut out the pattern pieces according to the pattern shown in Figure A.

SEWING AND STUFFING
Bi-Colored Boy—Sew together the upper and lower bodies, then sew the front to the back. You can also cut pattern as one piece. Overlap seam allowances in the middle, and make this doll from a single piece of fabric. Make suspenders with ribbon when the doll is finished.

Girl's Pinafore—Cut a piece of fabric 4 inches long and 13 inches wide for the skirt. Stitch a 1/2-inch hem at the bottom. Sew a 1/4-inch casing for elastic at the waist. Fold the fabric in half, with right-sides facing. Stitch the raw edges of the two shorter sides together. Turn the fabric right-side out before gathering the waist.

Gather the skirt, but do not secure gathers until the skirt is fitted on the girl. The gathered skirt will be permanently sewn to her body. You can also gather the skirt with elastic, see page 12, before attaching it to the doll. This makes the skirt removable.

For the pinafore top, wrap eyelet trim around her as shown in Figure B. Tack in place.

EMBROIDERY
See page 9 for information on embroidery stitches. Figures can be embroidered after being assembled and stuffed. You can do a neater job and correct mistakes by embroidering faces before joining the front and back of figures' bodies. See Figure C. The exception to this is the hair. Hair is added *after* the figure is sewn and stuffed. See Figures D and E.
Eyes—Use a satin-stitch.
Eyelashes and Brows—Use a straight-stitch.
Mouth—Use a chain-stitch.
Nose—Use a French knot for the boy and girl and a chain-stitch for the saguaro cactus.

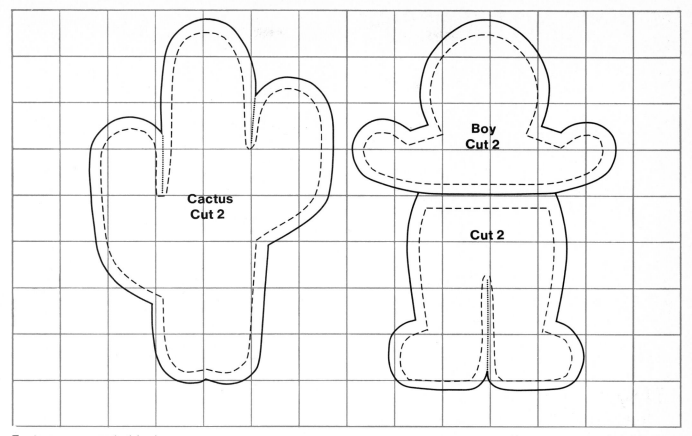

Each square equals 1 inch.

Cactus
Cut 2

Boy
Cut 2

Cut 2

Figure B—For variation, use lace trim or decorative ribbon for pinafore.

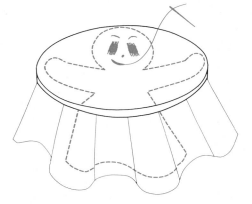

Figure C—Follow combination of stitches used here or make designs from stitches found on page 9.

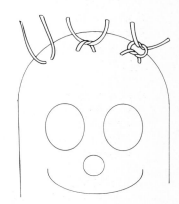

Figure D

Figure D—For top of saguaro, draw two or three strands of embroidery thread through fabric with a needle. Tie square knot, then clip.

Figure E—For children's hair, use three strands of floss to make random chain-stitch.

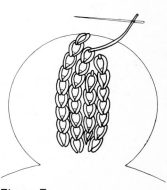

Figure E

Clutch Toys

The first toys to interest a baby are ones that are easy to grasp. Use fabric scraps to make homemade toys for baby. Be sure fabrics are safe, durable and machine-washable.

EQUIPMENT
- **Enlarging supplies, page 12**
- **Transferring supplies, page 20**
- **Sewing supplies**
- **Stuffing tool, page 18**

MATERIALS
- **Small scraps of washable fabric**
- **Thread to match**
- **Less than 1 bag of polyfill, page 18**
- **Embroidery thread, optional**

ENLARGING, TRANSFERRING, SEWING AND STUFFING

Enlarge the pattern, using the technique described on page 12. Cut out the pattern pieces according to the patterns.

Appliquéd House—Use one fabric for the front of the house and a different fabric for the back to create a unique toy. See Figure A. In this toy, the window and door fabric on one side was the background fabric for the other side. Windows and doors are appliquéd with a blanket-stitch, page 10. After stitching appliqués, sew edges together and stuff.

One Ball—Trace and cut 12 pieces of five-sided fabric. See Figure B. The ball is made in halves, so divide the pieces into six sets of two.

To make the first half, choose a central piece. Sew one edge of five other pieces to its five sides. See Figure C. Sew the side edges of the five pieces to each other to create a dish. See Figure D. Repeat this process with the other half of the ball.

Sew halves together to make the ball. Leave two sides open for stuffing. When you have stuffed the ball, sew the two open sides together. Leave as is or embroider around each pentagon. A chain-stitch was used on the ball shown here, but other stitches can be used, page 10.

Stuffed Circles—Cut three circles of fabric in any size. Mark the halfway point at both ends on the wrong-side of each circle. See Figure E. With right-sides facing, use the halfway point as a guide. Sew half of the first circle to half of the second circle, using a 1/4-inch seam. Leave a 1-1/2-inch opening. See Figure F.

Fold the top circle back. Match the third circle, face down, to the unsewn part of the first circle. See Figure F. Sew the halves together around the edge. Leave a 1-1/2-inch opening. Open ends should point in the same direction.

Sew the final halves of circles together. When pieces are assembled, turn the fabric right-side out. Arrange it so two circles are visible and one is folded in. Stitch down the center, from one half to the next. See Figure G for the seam line.

Arrange fabric so the circle with the seam is folded in and the unstitched circle is face up. Stitch down the center of this circle also. Stuff and close the gaps with a slip-stitch.

Hexagon Toys—Trace and cut 14 pieces of fabric from the six-sided pattern. See Figure H. The toy is made in halves, so divide the pieces into two sets of seven.

To make the first half, choose one central piece. Sew one edge of the other six pieces around it. See Figure C. Sew the edges of these six pieces to each other. See Figure D. Follow the same method for the second half.

When both parts are assembled, match them with right-sides together. Stitch around the edges, leaving two sides open for stuffing. Turn the toy right-side out, stuff it and close the gaps.

If you choose, embroider around the sections. You can also turn the shape into a character, such as a flower, the sun or in this case, a turtle.

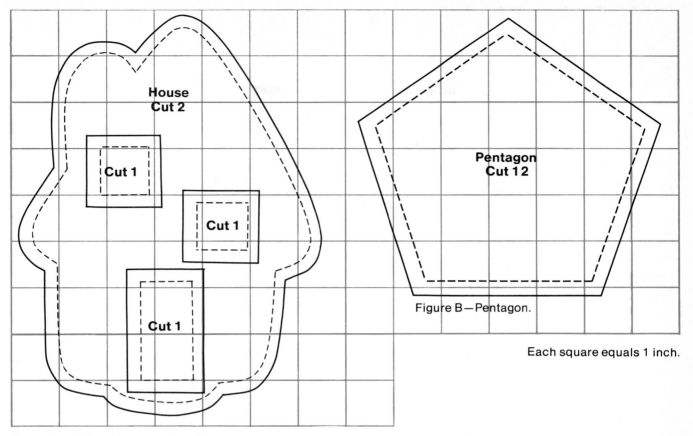

**House
Cut 2**

Cut 1

Cut 1

Cut 1

**Pentagon
Cut 12**

Figure B—Pentagon.

Each square equals 1 inch.

Figure A—This pattern was traced from a cookie cutter.

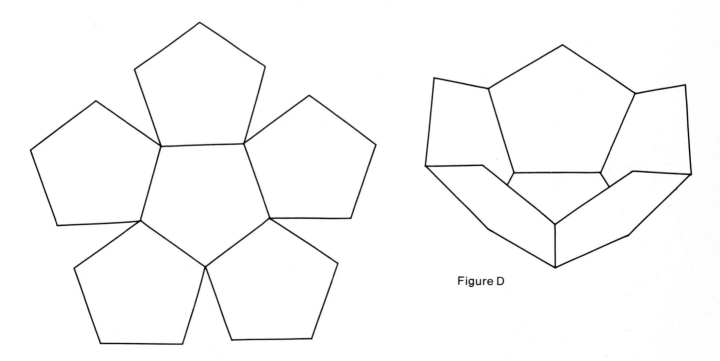

Figure D

Figure C—While a pentagon and hexagon differ in the number of sides, ball and hexagon toy are made the same way.

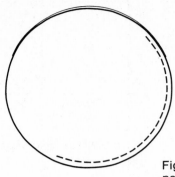

Figure E—Enlarge this circle or make one with a compass or trace something round.

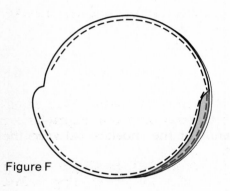

Figure F

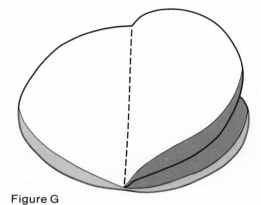

Figure G

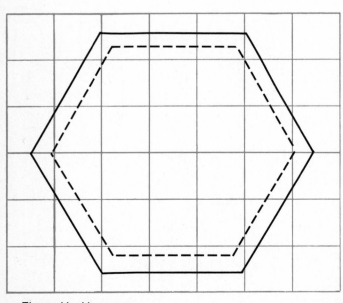

Figure H—Hexagon.
Each square equals 1 inch.

To make a hexagon bath toy, use terry cloth and stuff with shredded foam.

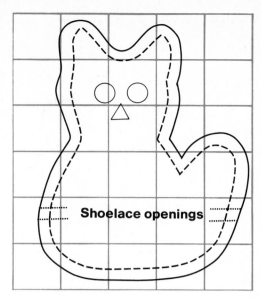

Figure A—Try this pattern or trace one from a cookie cutter.

Each square equals 1 inch.

Three-Kittens Crib Toy

An infant will enjoy studying these bright characters. The crib toy is fastened to the crib, bassinet or playpen with shoelaces. If desired, you can add bells to the stuffing. The same pattern is used for the Cat Mobile, page 121.

EQUIPMENT
- **Enlarging supplies, page 12**
- **Sewing supplies**
- **Stuffing tool, page 18**
- **Embroidery hoop, optional, page 21**

MATERIALS
- **1 pair of shoelaces, at least 18 inches long**
- **Less than 1/3 yard of 45-inch-wide washable fabric**
- **Small amount of embroidery thread to make faces and collars**
- **1 bag of polyfill, page 18**
- **Bells, optional**

ENLARGING, TRANSFERRING, SEWING AND STUFFING

Enlarge the pattern, using the technique described on page 12. Cut out the pattern pieces according to the pattern shown in Figure A.

Embroidering—Embroider features on the kittens before doing the final sewing. See page 9 for information on embroidery stitches. Use a back-stitch for the features and a chain-stitch for the collar.

Attaching Ties—Fold one shoelace in half to determine its length. You need 9 inches on each side for fastening. If shoelaces are longer, cut them in equal pieces. See Figure B. Cut off plastic ends.

Shoelaces are sewn in the seam. Place right-sides of fabric together and pin edges. Before sewing, tuck ends of the shoelace between the pieces of fabric.

Stuffing and Attaching Kittens—Begin stuffing the kittens. Add bells to the stuffing before stitching is complete. When you have stuffed each kitten, close the opening with a slip-stitch. Sew kittens together as shown in photo.

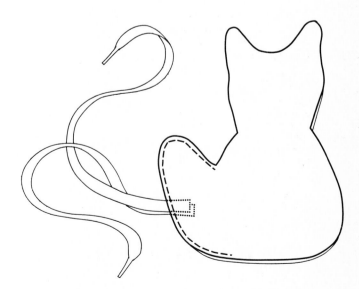

Figure B—Cut off plastic ends. When toy is sewn and turned right-side out, long ends are ready to tie.

MAKING DOLL

Enlarge the pattern, using the technique described on page 12. Cut out the pattern pieces according to the patterns shown in Figures A, B, C and D. With right-sides facing, pin two feet together. Stitch from the top of the center back to the top of center front.

Fold the leg according to the pattern. Match center fronts, and stitch the foot to the leg. Stitch the center-back seam from the upper edge to the top back of the shoe. Complete the leg. See Figure B. With right-sides facing, pin and sew two arms together. Leave upper edges open. Repeat for the other arm.

With right-sides facing, sew the front of the body to the back. Leave openings for arms and legs at the points where you want to insert them. Clip into the curves of the arms, legs and body. Turn all parts right-side out.

Using a stuffing tool for the tips of the toes, stuff the lower legs. Stitch across the leg to make the knee, as shown in the pattern. See Figure B. Lightly stuff the rest of the leg. Fold upper raw edges under, and baste the top seam. Follow the same procedure for the arms.

To join arms to the body, turn under raw edges on the body openings and press. Slip an arm in an opening, and stitch in place through all thicknesses. Repeat for the other arm and both legs. Leave an opening at the bottom edge of the body for stuffing.

Generously stuff the body. Turn under the raw edge and close the gap. Make hair with yarn. See Figure D, page 87.

Sleepy Clown

A small baby will love to look at the face and pull the hair of this sleepy clown. A toddler will learn to undress and later, dress him. This sturdy companion is washable.

EQUIPMENT
- Enlarging supplies, page 12
- Sewing supplies
- Stuffing tool, page 18

MATERIALS
- 1/2 yard of 45-inch-wide broadcloth or other washable fabric for the body
- 1 yard of 45-inch-wide polyester-blend or lightweight stretch fabric for the outfit
- 1/4 yard of 45-inch-wide fabric for shoes
- Thread to match fabric
- Small scraps of felt
- Small amount of yarn
- 1 hook and eye

MAKING OUTFIT

Enlarge the pattern, using the technique described on page 12. Cut out the pattern pieces according to the pattern shown in Figure E. For the ruffle, make a 2-1/2x12-1/2'' rectangle. Add a 1/4-inch seam allowance on all sides. Cut four pieces to make the outfit and cut one ruffle.

For the front of the costume, match two pieces with right-sides together. Sew from the crotch to the facing, as shown by the dots in Figure F. For the back of the costume, stitch from the crotch to the neck. Next, match the front and back pieces, with right-sides together. Sew around the edges, leaving openings at the hands, feet and neck. Turn the raw edge of the neck to the inside and stitch. Add elastic. See Figure G and page 9.

Make a ruffle, page 17. Adjust fullness as you pin the ruffle to the outfit. Baste the ruffle to the outfit with raw edges on the wrong-side. Topstitch in place, and fold the ruffle over the neck.

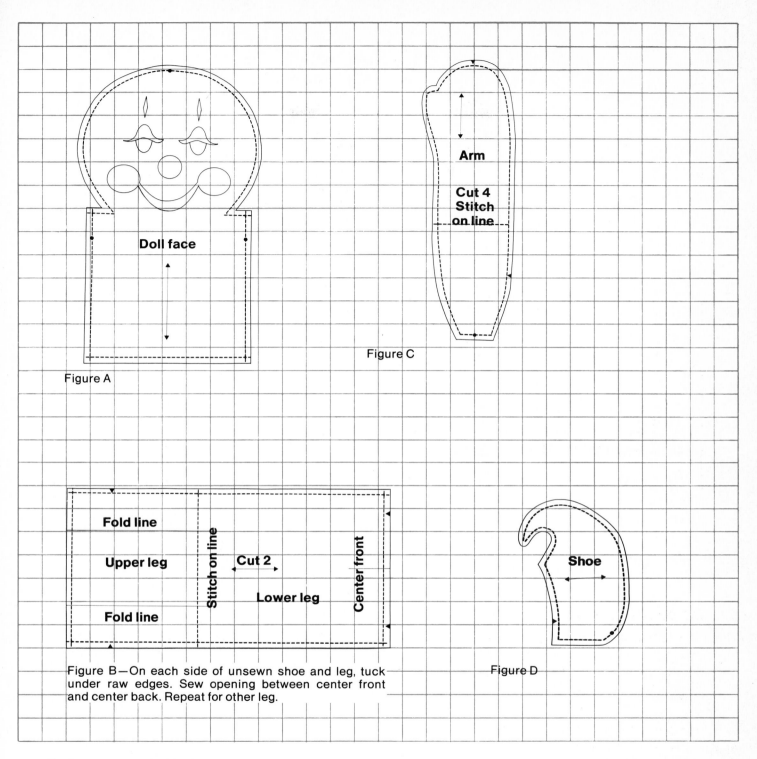

Doll face

Figure A

Arm

**Cut 4
Stitch
on line**

Figure C

Fold line

Upper leg

Stitch on line

Cut 2

Lower leg

Center front

Fold line

Shoe

Figure D

Figure B—On each side of unsewn shoe and leg, tuck under raw edges. Sew opening between center front and center back. Repeat for other leg.

Each square equals 1 inch.

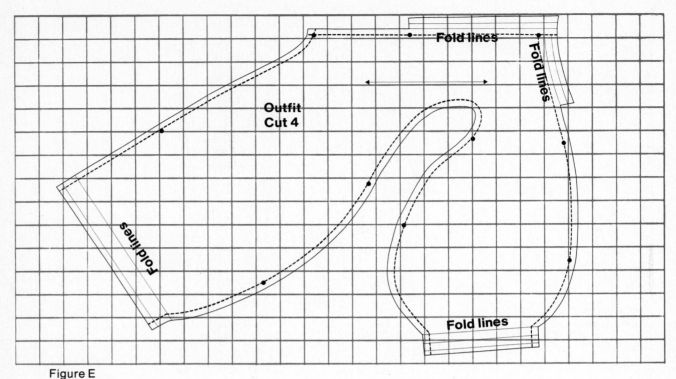

Outfit
Cut 4

Fold lines

Fold lines

Fold lines

Fold lines

Figure E

Each square equals 1 inch.

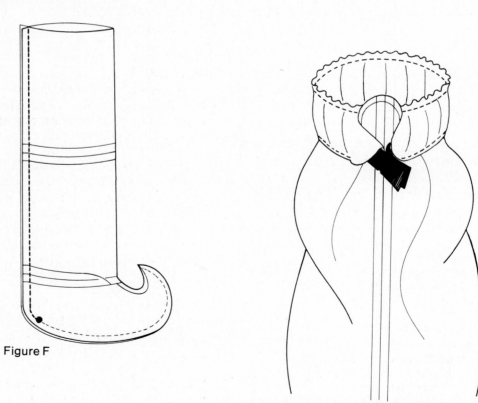

Figure F

Figure G—Finish lower edge of sleeve with wide hem to allow for width of elastic. Leave opening at the seam. Edge-stitch lower edge. Insert elastic to fit wrist. Lap ends of elastic, sew together and close opening.

Yarn Dolls

Made from yarn and pantyhose or stockings, these cuddly dolls can be machine-washed with wonderful results. The button eyes and nose are stitched under the face, covered by a layer of fabric. This makes the toy especially safe and durable.

EQUIPMENT
- Enlarging supplies, page 12
- 1 piece of cardboard, 11x14″
- Sewing supplies

MATERIALS FOR ONE DOLL
- 1/2 skein of yarn
- 2 pairs of pantyhose, with two usable feet
- 1/2 yard of 45-inch-wide stretchy, nylon fabric
- Embroidery thread to match
- 1/2 yard of 45-inch-wide flannel or fabric with a soft nap
- Thread to match fabric
- 3 buttons for eyes and nose
- Few strands of yarn for hair, optional

MAKING DOLL

To make the body, wind yarn around the 14-inch side of the cardboard 150 times. Tie loose strands to adjoining ones. Tie both ends with a 12-inch piece of yarn. Slip yarn off the cardboard.

With a single piece of yarn, tie off a section 4 inches from the top. This is for the head. Untie the piece used to slip yarn off the top end of cardboard.

To make the arms, wind yarn around the 11-inch side 50 times. Tie the first and last strands to adjoining ones. Tie the two ends with a 12-inch piece of yarn. Slip yarn off the cardboard.

Slip the arms through the body, and tie the waist. Next, tie the hands. Untie the piece at the bottom of the body, and divide the yarn into two legs. Tie the feet. See Figure A.

Cut the feet off the stockings. Stuff 4 inches of one with shredded hose. The form of this determines the shape of the head, so pack it carefully and solidly. Add extra padding at the cheeks. Tie under the stuffed piece and slip the piece between the yarn, through the back of the doll's head.

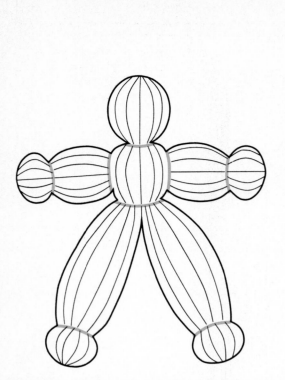

Figure A—To find out where to tie yarn in sections, compare doll to pattern for outfit.

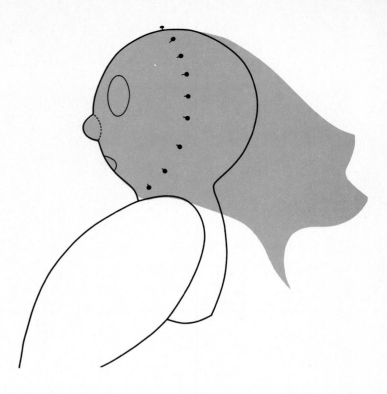

Figure B—Stretch fabric is pulled tightly over the head and sewn in place.

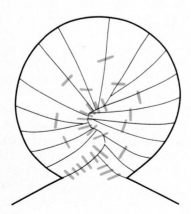

Figure C—Stitches to tuck and fold material will not be seen.

Arrange yarn around the inserted head piece so there is little separation, especially on what will be the face. Cover the head with the second stocking foot, and rearrange separated yarn. Continue working the stuffed head until the desired shape is achieved. Tie off at the neck. Sew buttons on the face for eyes and a nose. Stitch as deeply as possible in the head with each stitch.

Arrange stretch fabric over the head. Pull it tightly across the face, smoothing wrinkles. Hold the fabric in place with straight pins. Outline the eyes and nose with a back-stitch. Stitch as deeply as possible in the head. See Figure B. Make a French knot or use another embroidery stitch for the mouth. Hair is added when the doll is almost complete.

Keep the stretch fabric wrinkle-free by smoothing it as you put it on. Fold it in a triangle on the back of the head and cut off excess bulk. Sew in place. The hood of the outfit is permanently attached to the doll. Stitches to make the folds in the fabric are not seen. See Figure C.

Tie loose fabric around the neck in place with a piece of yarn. Stitch all around, slightly above the yarn. On the front, make the stitch low enough to be concealed by the outfit.

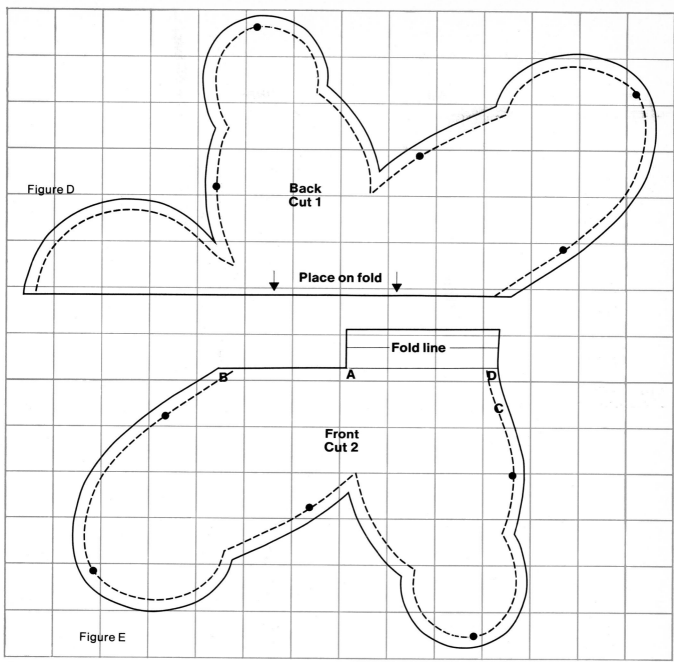

Figure D

Back
Cut 1

Place on fold

Fold line

B   A   D
          C

Front
Cut 2

Figure E

Each square equals 1 inch.

MAKING OUTFIT

Enlarge the pattern, using the technique described on page 12. Cut out the pattern pieces according to the pattern shown in Figure A. Cut one back piece, two front pieces and one rectangular piece for the hat. Cut the hat 6x10-1/4. With right-sides facing, stitch together the front pieces from the crotch to the facing. With right-sides facing, sew the front to the back. For the opening, finish the facing. On one side, fold the raw edges under 1/4 inch and press. Fold under 1/4 inch again, press and machine- or hand-stitch. See the markings in Figure A. Repeat this for the other side.

Fold the hat piece in half lengthwise. Center it on the head part of the back piece. With right-sides together, sew the two pieces together with a running-stitch, page 11. Fit the hat on the doll as you go along by easing and gathering the fabric. See page 12 for information on gathering. Secure the running-stitch by sewing over it with the machine or an overcasting-stitch, page 11.

Put the outfit on the doll. Before sewing the hat to the head, add the hair. With right-sides together, stitch the hat from one side to the next.

Close the opening with a slip-stitch or more-decorative embroidery-stitch. Slightly gather the hands and feet with a running-stitch.

Action Toys

The activity toys in this section involve infants and toddlers in play and learning. The *Crib Exerciser*, page 99, encourages an infant to bat and pull. The *Snappy Turtle*, page 104, teaches the child how to open and close various openings. Projects use different construction techniques, such as macramé, sewing, gluing and simple woodworking.

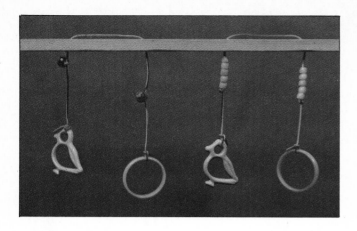

Crib Exerciser

This is a great toy for an infant or older baby. An infant can exercise by batting at it. An older baby can pull it, creating sound and movement. One side of the exerciser has bells that jingle. The other side has beads that clack against the wood base.

EQUIPMENT
- Hand or electric drill
- 1/4-inch and 3/8-inch wood bits

MATERIAL
- 1 piece of 1x2 fir or pine, 24 inches long
- Non-toxic, clear wood finish or stain
- 1 pair leather boot laces, 72 inches long
- 10 wood beads, 1/2 inch in diameter
- 2 bells
- 2 teething rings or rattles
- 2 plastic costume-jewelry bracelets
- Medium-grit and fine-grit sandpaper

MAKING TOY

Drill four 1/4-inch and four 3/8-inch holes in the board, using Figure A as a guide. Sand wood lightly in the direction of the grain. Wood can be finished with a clear finish or non-toxic color stain.

Cut two 24-inch pieces and two 30-inch pieces of boot lace. Put the ends of one 24-inch piece of lace through each pair of 1/4-inch holes. Pull the ends through until they are even. Tie a square

knot, page 100. Tie the end of one of the 30-inch pieces of lace on a plastic bracelet. Use a double-half hitch, page 101. Seven inches above the bracelet, tie an overhand knot. See Figure B.

String five wood beads on the lace. Bring the lace up through the end of hole 1. Feed the lace down through hole 2. See Figure A. String five wood beads on the lace and tie an overhand knot 7 inches above the end of the lace. Attach one of the teething rings to the lace with a double-half hitch.

Thread one bell on the other 30-inch piece of boot lace. Tie in place 9 inches from the end, using an overhand knot. See Figure C. Tie the end of the lace to the second bracelet with a double-half hitch.

Bring the second boot lace up through hole 3 and down through hole 4. See Figure A. Attach another bell 9 inches above this end using an overhand knot. See Figure C. Attach the remaining teething ring to the other end with a double-half-hitch knot.

Use the two 24-inch pieces of boot lace to suspend the toy above the crib. Tie one piece of lace to one crib rail and the other piece to the opposite crib rail. Baby can bat at it or pull on it.

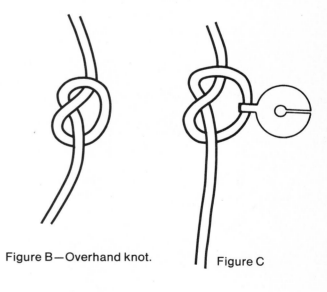

Figure B—Overhand knot.　　　Figure C

3/4"	4-1/2"	4-1/2"	4-1/2"	4-1/2"	4-1/2"	3/4"

Figure A—The two holes at each end are 1/4 inch. The four holes in the middle are 3/8 inch. Drawing not actual size.

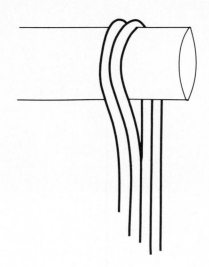

Figure A—Use a dowel or cardboard tube.

Beads on Boot Laces

This toy can be attached to a stroller or car seat, or baby can carry it around. Make it quickly and inexpensively. Boot laces are great for baby's teething.

EQUIPMENT
- 1 wood dowel or cardboard tube, 2 inches in diameter

MATERIALS
- 1 pair of braided or leather boot laces, 72 inches long
- 4 oval wood beads, 2 inches in diameter
- 4 round wood beads, 1 inch in diameter

EQUIPMENT
Place the pair of boot laces over the dowel or tube, keeping ends even. See Figure A. Tie two square knots as shown in Figure B. Put the first oval wood bead on the holding cord. Tie four reversed double-half hitches. See Figure D.

Put all four cords through the first round wood bead, and tie a square knot. Put the second oval wood bead on the holding cord, and tie two square knots. Put all four cords through the second round bead. Tie six alternating half hitches. See Figure E.

Run two cords through the third oval bead from the left and two cords through the same bead from the right. See Figure F. Tie four alternating half hitches. See Figure E.

Put all four cords through the third round

Figure B—Square knot is made of two half knots. One knot goes left, the other goes right. Four cords are used. Two center cords are known as the *holding cord* and are held taut until knot is complete.

bead, and tie a square knot. Put the fourth oval bead on the holding cord. Tie two square knots. Put all four cords through the fourth round bead. Tie four double chain knots. See Figure G. Follow these knots with two square knots. If using braided laces, cut plastic tips.

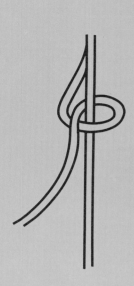

Figure C—Half hitch forms basis for many other knots, such as the double-chain knot. See Figure G.

Figure D—Reversed double-half hitch.

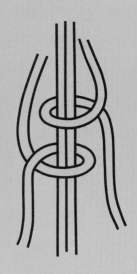

Figure E—Alternating half hitches.

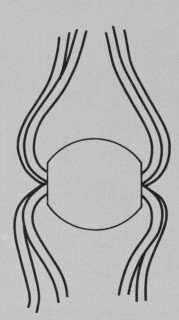

Figure F

Figure G—Double-chain knots.

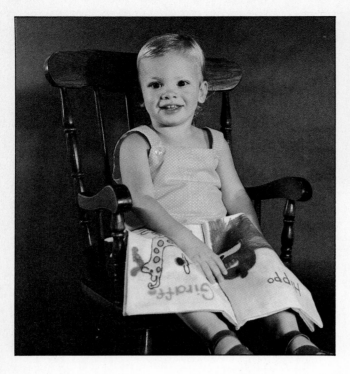

Cloth Books

One way to teach a baby language is by naming things in picture books. In these cloth books, picture contents can be appliquéd or drawn. The sturdy pages will endure many readings and machine-washings.

EQUIPMENT
- **Sewing supplies**
- **Colored pencil**
- **Ruler, page 20**
- **Embroidery hoop, if making appliquéd version**
- **Newspaper for work area, if using fabric markers**
- **Fabric markers, page 20**

MATERIALS
- **3/4 to 1 yard of 45-inch-wide fabric**
- **Appliqués. Number depends on the number of pages in the book.**
- **Embroidery thread**

DESIGNING BOOK
The size and number of pages and the size of the cover will vary. You can make the book in any size. The books shown in the photograph are 9x8" and 9-1/2x7-1/2". Less than 3/4 yard of fabric was needed for each. Any polyester-blend fabric can be used for the pages. Make the cover from a heavier material if you include quilted appliqués. Heavier fabric gives body to the book.

If you draw pictures with fabric markers, make the entire book from light-color, heavy fabric, such as sailcloth. If you make an appliquéd cloth book, you can design your own appliqués, see page 5, or use ready-made appliqués. Ready-made appliqués were used with the *Love Book*. Sew appliqués with a zigzag-stitch or by hand with embroidery floss.

ASSEMBLING BOOK
Make a rectangle twice the width you want each page to be. The rectangle will be your template. See page 15 for information on making templates. Cut out the pattern piece according to the illustration shown in Figure A. The same template is used for both the cover and pages. Different seam allowances are added as you trace the pattern on fabric. The cover must be bigger than the pages, so add a 1/4-inch seam allowance on all four sides. This allows the two rectangles to be used for the cover. Allow a 3/4-inch seam allowance for pages. See Figure A. Cut one, two or as many sets of rectangles as you want for pages. The book will be bulky when it is bound.

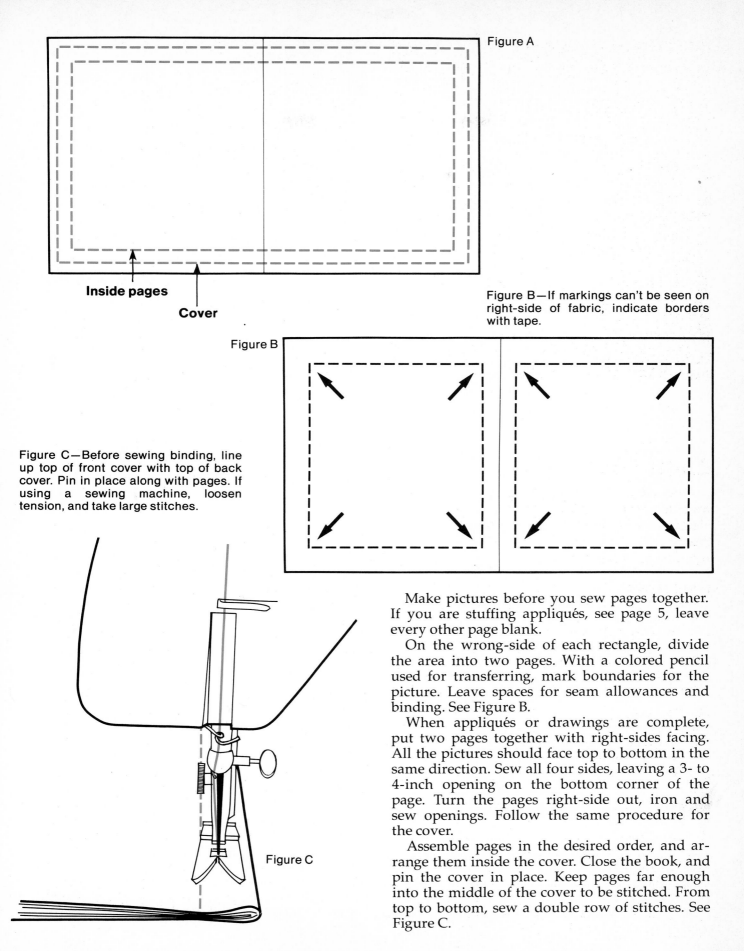

Figure A

Inside pages

Cover

Figure B—If markings can't be seen on right-side of fabric, indicate borders with tape.

Figure B

Figure C—Before sewing binding, line up top of front cover with top of back cover. Pin in place along with pages. If using a sewing machine, loosen tension, and take large stitches.

Figure C

Make pictures before you sew pages together. If you are stuffing appliqués, see page 5, leave every other page blank.

On the wrong-side of each rectangle, divide the area into two pages. With a colored pencil used for transferring, mark boundaries for the picture. Leave spaces for seam allowances and binding. See Figure B.

When appliqués or drawings are complete, put two pages together with right-sides facing. All the pictures should face top to bottom in the same direction. Sew all four sides, leaving a 3- to 4-inch opening on the bottom corner of the page. Turn the pages right-side out, iron and sew openings. Follow the same procedure for the cover.

Assemble pages in the desired order, and arrange them inside the cover. Close the book, and pin the cover in place. Keep pages far enough into the middle of the cover to be stitched. From top to bottom, sew a double row of stitches. See Figure C.

Puppet attached with Velcro can be enjoyed by children of all ages.

Snappy Turtle

This multiple-use learning toy teaches a baby about pockets, a toddler about buttons and snaps, and a young child about shoelaces. The turtle's head, attached to the shell with Velcro, is also a puppet.

EQUIPMENT
- Enlarging supplies, page 12
- Sewing supplies
- Stuffing tool, page 18
- Eyelet kit

MATERIALS
- 1/2 yard of 45-inch-wide polyester-blend fabric in one color
- 1/2 yard of 45-inch-wide polyester-blend fabric in a second color
- Thread to match fabric
- 1 sheet of felt for baby turtles
- Embroidery thread for features on baby turtles
- Buttons for the puppet's eyes and nose
- 4 sets of decorative buttons
- 1 yard of yarn to match fabric
- 2 sets of snaps
- 10 inches of Velcro
- 1 shoelace, 18 inches long
- Scraps of felt, vinyl or ribbon for tongue and eyebrows
- 2 circles of polyester batting, 13-1/2 inches in circumference
- Small amount of batting for turtles
- 1 bell, optional

MAKING SHELL
Enlarge all patterns, using the technique described on page 12. Cut out the pattern pieces according to the pattern shown in Figure A. For the shell, make two 14-1/2-inch circles. Cut two 13-1/2-inch circles from batting.

Iron seams to the wrong-side on the fabric circles. With the right-sides of the fabric on the outside, place the two circles of batting between them. Pin the layers in place. With a machine- or back-stitch, page 9, stitch the circles together 1/4 inch inside the edge. Sew another seam 5/8 inch inside the edge.

Cut three pockets. For the opening side, stitch under the raw edge. For pocket edges sewn on the shell, tuck under raw edges. Clip into curves and iron in place. With straight pins or a basting-stitch, page 9, attach pockets to the shell. Sew in place with a zigzag-stitch on the sewing machine or use a hand buttonhole-stitch, page 10.

MAKING BABY TURTLES
Trace and cut six turtles from felt. See Figure B. This pattern does not have to be enlarged. With a running- or back-stitch, sew two turtles together. Leave a small opening for stuffing, then stuff the turtles.

Fold the 1-yard piece of yarn into three equal pieces and cut it. Tuck the end of one piece in the seam. Close the opening. Make the eyes and nose with a French knot. Decorate the shell with a lazy-daisy-stitch, page 11. Repeat for the other turtles. Inside the pocket, near the bottom seam, sew the other end of the yarn in place with thread to match pocket.

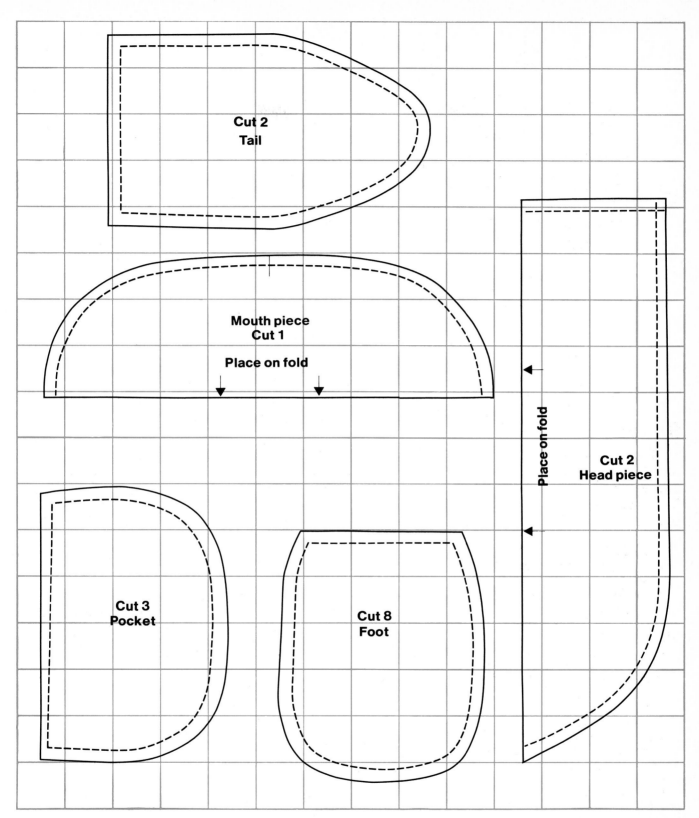

Figure A
Each square equals 1 inch.

MAKING LEGS AND TAIL

Cut two tails and eight feet. With right-sides facing, sew around each foot. Leave the top open for stuffing. Turn right-side out. Stuff to within 3/4 inch from the top. Sew along the center line with a machine- or back-stitch.

Tuck in the raw edges of the open end and stitch together. When making the tail, stuff to within 1-1/2 inches of the opening. If desired, include a bell.

When closing the opening, stitch a rectangle 1/4 inch in the seam, 1-1/2 inches deep. This un-stuffed area is used for eyelets.

ADDING ATTACHMENTS

Before allowing baby to play with the toy, securely sew buttons and snaps. Check them periodically for looseness when the toy is in use. Sew a pair of decorative buttons on two of the feet. Sew the bottom halves of two sets of snaps to the other feet. Line up the feet with the shell, alternating snaps with buttons. Sew the top of the snaps to the underside of the shell between the circular seams. On the top of the shell, where the two sets of stitches can be seen, sew decorative buttons.

For the button attachments, make buttonholes between the circular seams. Sew with a machine- or buttonhole-stitch, page 10.

Following instructions on the eyelet kit, punch six holes. Attach two sets of eyelets to the tail and one set between the circular seams on the shell. Attach the tail to the shell by lacing with the shoelace.

MAKING PUPPET

Cut two head pieces and one mouth. For the features, you can also cut a tongue and eyebrows, but they are optional. On one head piece, sew eyes and eyebrows. With right-sides together, sew the top of the head piece to the top half of the mouth piece. See Figure C.

When the mouth piece is attached, turn it right-side out. Align it under the shell to determine the position of the Velcro. Sew Velcro to what will be the top half of the puppet. Turn the puppet inside out, and sew the sides of the turtle's neck. Leave an open end for the hand. End the seam 1/2 inch from the raw edge.

Fold the raw edges under 1/4 inch and press. Fold under 1/4 inch again, press and machine- or hand-stitch. Sew the tongue inside the mouth with a back-stitch. Add the button for a nose.

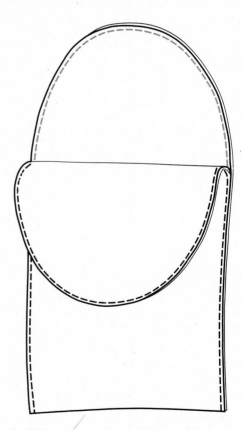

Figure C—With right-sides together, sew top half of underside piece to unsewn half of mouth piece.

Figure B—Trace this pattern and use the same size.

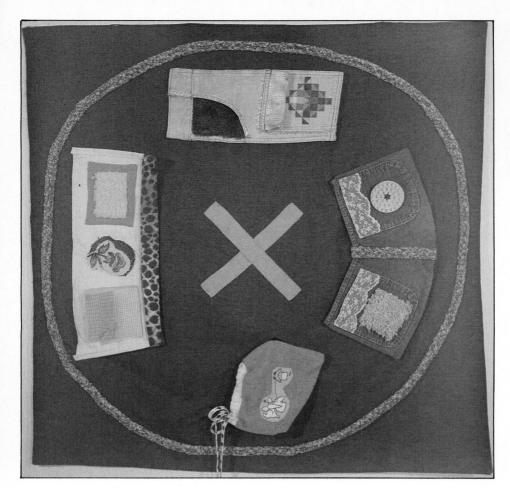

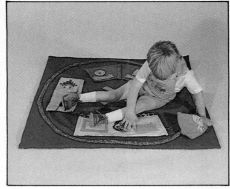

A child has many textures to explore, in or out of the playpen.

Texture Pad

This pad will let baby play with a variety of textures and pockets while spending time in the playpen. Pockets for this pad are made from old jeans, the hood of a worn-out jacket and a carpenter's apron. Among the textures sewn on the pockets are a swatch of carpet and a soap holder. The circle is made from a discarded sweater. Ribbing from the sweater was cut in strips and sewn together.

EQUIPMENT
- Yardstick or measuring tape, page 20
- Fabric marker, page 20
- Sewing supplies

MATERIALS
- 2-1/2 yards of 45-inch-wide denim or other heavy, washable fabric
- 1 standard-size playpen pad, 3x3'

Or

- 3/4- to 1-inch foam, covered with plastic

MAKING PAD
Materials for this pad will be touched and probably tasted by baby. Be selective in your choices. Avoid abrasive materials, such as sandpaper, and sharp objects. If you use buttons, sew them on securely, and check them often for looseness. If adding hand-washable fabrics, sew them on one or two removable pockets.

The playpen cover is made the same way as the *Pad Cover*, page 42, with the following exception. Velcro strips and other materials sewn on the top are attached before joining top and bottom pieces.

Covered Shape Box

This shape sorter is a sturdy cardboard box hinged with packing tape and covered with a single piece of fabric. It develops eye-hand coordination. A child will enjoy opening and closing the lid as much as dropping objects through the holes.

EQUIPMENT
- **Razor blade**
- **Or**
- **Scissors for craft work, page 20**
- **Pencil**
- **Tool for spreading glue, page 13**
- **Covering for work area**
- **Measuring tape, page 20**
- **Paper for pattern**
- **Cookie cutters for animals, optional**

MATERIALS
- **1 sturdy cardboard box, such as a gift box**
- **Fabric, amount varies. For this box, which measures 4-1/8x7-1/8", 3/4 yard of 45-inch-wide fabric was needed.**
- **Packing tape**
- **Felt for the inside top of box, amount varies**
- **White glue or spray adhesive**
- **Decorative felt, lace trim and rickrack, optional**

PREPARING BOX

A baby will be handling the toy, so the box should not be too big or too small. If the box is too big, it is difficult to handle. If too small, the wood pegs are also small. They could be a safety hazard if the baby got one lodged in his throat.

Cut one side of the box rim off the lid with scissors or razor blade. Trace the bottom of the pegs on the box lid. Directions for making pegs can be found with the *Wood Blocks*, page 111. With a blade, cut holes 1/4 inch larger than the size of the pegs. Before gluing fabric to the box, tape the cut side of the lid to both sides of the box with long strips of packing tape.

MAKING PATTERN

To make a pattern, see Figure A. The box will be covered with fabric on all sides. Take all measurements before you cut out a paper pattern. Measure the bottom of the box. Add 1/8 inch to this measurement. If the bottom measures 7-1/8 inches, make your pattern pieces 7-1/4 inches.

Measure one side of the box, and double this measurement. Do not double the measurement of the side leading to the lid of the box. The double measurement for the side of the box includes material for covering the inside of the box. See Figure A. Add a 1/2-inch seam allowance on all sides.

Measure the bottom of the box for fabric to cover the inside bottom. See Figure A, section 4. For the last side, add 1/2 inch in length to the measurement so fabric overlaps on the inside lid. See Figure B. Instead of allowing 1/2 inch for the finished seam on these sections, allow a 1/4-inch seam.

Measure the outside lid. See Figure A. Measure one side of the outside rim, and double the measurement. Add a 1/4-inch seam allowance on all three sides. See Figures A and B. Using the measurements and following the illustration in Figure A, draw a paper pattern of the correct proportions. Cut one piece of fabric according to the paper pattern.

GLUING BOX

Put a cover over your work area. Lay the fabric you are using to cover the box wrong-side up. Before gluing the fabric to the box, consider this. When covering the box, you must keep white glue from clumping and showing through the fabric. You must also make sure all the fabric is glued down. Except for seams, which are discussed later, the easiest way to do this is to apply glue to the box. Glue can be put on one section at a time. If using spray adhesive, spray the box and fabric at the same time. Adhesive remains tacky for a long period. This allows time to work with it.

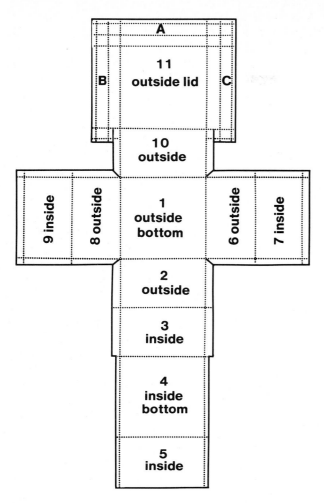

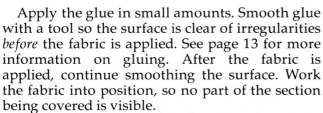

Figure A—Before cutting fabric, wrap your box in paper pattern to check measurements. Practice covering procedure.

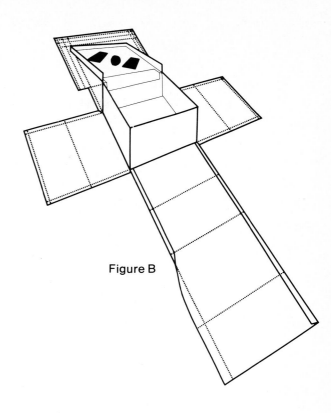

Figure B

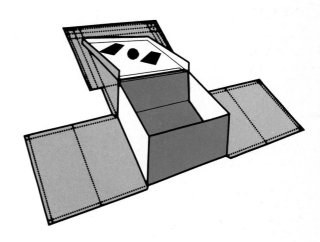

Figure C

Apply the glue in small amounts. Smooth glue with a tool so the surface is clear of irregularities *before* the fabric is applied. See page 13 for more information on gluing. After the fabric is applied, continue smoothing the surface. Work the fabric into position, so no part of the section being covered is visible.

Begin by gluing fabric to the bottom of the box. See Figure A, section 1. Work with sections 2 through 5, as shown in Figure A. Before gluing the sections in sequence, finish the seams on both sides of the long strip that covers the front, bottom and top of the box.

Fold the strip and apply glue to the raw edges. If necessary, adjust the folds to fit the box. When this step is complete, apply glue on the outside of section 2. Apply glue to the inside of section 3, to the inside bottom of section 4 and to the inside leading up to and slightly overlapping the lid, in section 5. See Figure B.

Next glue the sides, sections 6 through 9. Fold the raw edges and apply glue. Turn under a hem before gluing fabric to the cardboard. See Figure C on previous page. Proceed the same way with side-section 10, which leads to the lid.

It is important for the lid to be wrinkle-free. Carefully lay the box on its side, and center the lid on the fabric. Fold the material over the rim so mitered corners are on the sides, not the front of the box. See page 14 for information about mitered corners.

Apply glue to the outside and inside of the rim. Pull the fabric over it. No hem is necessary because felt will be used to cover the raw edges. Fold sides, miter corners and tuck the tabs between the outside rim and fabric. See Figures D and E.

Leave the open box on its side. Cut holes for pegs through the fabric with a blade. See Figure F. For gluing cut fabric to the inside lid, see the *Covered Frames*, page 150.

Cut felt the same size as the inside lid. Before gluing the felt, trace the holes from the top side of the lid onto the felt. Cut them out. Apply glue to the box instead of the fabric. Glue felt to the inside lid.

Make pegs for the box. See instructions in the *Wood Blocks*, page 111. Decorate the completed box. The one shown in the photograph is decorated with felt, lace and rickrack. The bird pattern can be found with the *Welcome-Baby Wreath*, page 140.

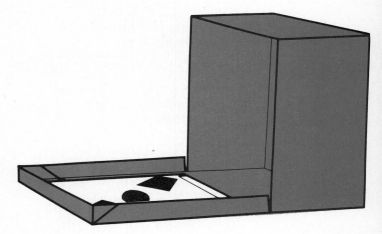

Figure E

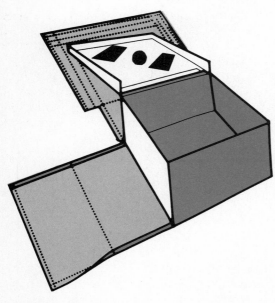

Figure D

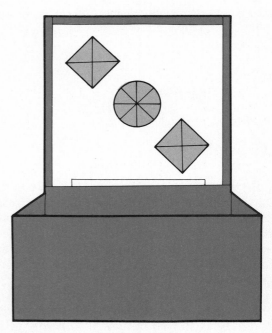

Figure F —By dividing and slashing holes in triangles, fabric over openings maintains original shape. See *Covered Frames*, page 150.

Interest in making castles and forts usually happens in preschool years, but baby can begin exploring individual shapes and weights.

Wood Blocks

Wood blocks are as traditional to the toy box as the quilt is to the layette. A set of blocks can be made from a softwood, such as fir or pine, and stained like these. They can also be made from hardwood, such as birch or maple, and sealed with clear sealant.

EQUIPMENT
- **Measuring tape or ruler, page 20**
- **Handsaw**
- **Miter box, optional**

MATERIALS
- **1 piece of 2x3, 24 inches long**
- **1 piece of 1x2, 24 inches long**
- **1 piece of 2x2, 24 inches long**
- **12-inch length of 1-1/2-inch-diameter wood closet pole**
- **Sandpaper, No. 120 grit**
- **Non-toxic wood stain or clear finish**

MAKING BLOCKS

Different sizes of lumber are needed to make a variety of blocks. Scrap lumber can be used, so check with lumberyards and home improvement centers. Ask permission to look through their scrap bins.

Be sure wood pieces are free of dirt, grease or wax. Out of the 2x3, cut two 6-inch pieces and four 3-inch pieces. Out of the 1x2, cut four 4-inch pieces and four 2-inch pieces.

Cut the closet pole into four 3-inch pieces to make pegs. Sand the pieces in the direction of the grain. Be sure there are no rough edges or corners. Remove dust from the blocks and apply stain or sealant, following directions.

Pegs and blocks can be made in any size to fit the *Covered Shape Box*, page 108.

Pull Toy

Screw eyes attach to the bottom of this pull toy to hold the dowels and bead wheels in place. There's plenty of clearance for the toy to be pulled over the thickest carpets and rockiest roads.

EQUIPMENT
- Handsaw
- Hand or power drill
- 2 pairs slip-joint pliers

MATERIALS
- 1 piece of 2x2 fir or pine, 9 inches long
- 1 piece of 1x2 fir or pine, 7 inches long
- 13 round, wood beads, 1-1/2 inches in diameter with a 3/8-inch center hole
- 12 No. 10 screw eyes
- 5 small screw eyes, with 1/4-inch shank
- 1 piece of 3/8-inch wood dowel, 26 inches long
- 1 oval-shape wood bead, 2 inches long
- 36 inches of cord or leather thong
- Non-toxic stain or paint
- 1 pair movable eyes
- Non-toxic enamel paint to draw eyes
- Non-toxic woodworker's glue
- Fine-grade sandpaper

MAKING PULL TOY

Cut the 2x2 in one 5-inch piece and one 4-inch piece. Cut the 1x2 in one 5-inch piece and one 2-inch piece. Cut the dowel in six 4-inch pieces and one 2-inch piece.

Use Figure A to determine the position of holes to be drilled. Drill pilot holes on the bottom of the 4- and 5-inch pieces of 2x2 and the 5-inch piece of the 1x2. Use a drill bit slightly smaller than the threads of the No. 10 screw eyes.

On the top of the 5-inch piece of 2x2, drill a hole 3/8 inch in diameter, 1/2 inch deep. This will hold the smokestack in place. Center the hole 1-1/2 inches from the front.

After drilling holes, sand all wood pieces until smooth. Center the 2-inch piece of 1x2 on the top of the 4-inch piece of 2x2. Glue it in place. Glue a 2-inch piece of dowel in the hole on the top of the 5-inch piece of 2x2. Glue oval wood bead on the dowel. Set the pieces aside and allow glue to dry.

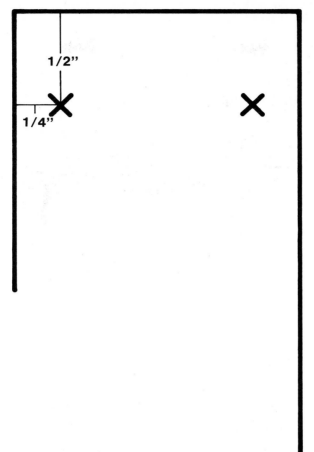

1/2"

1/4"

Figure A—Hole placement for pull toy. The other side is a mirror image of this one.

After glue has dried, paint or stain the pieces different colors. In the photograph, the 5-inch piece of 2x2 is stained yellow, the 4-inch piece of 2x2 is red and the 5-inch piece of 1x2 is blue. Two of the 4-inch pieces of dowel are stained red, two yellow and two blue.

When stain is dry, insert a No. 10 screw eye in each pilot hole you drilled on the bottom of the wood pieces. Glue a different-color bead on the end of each dowel. In the example shown here, orange beads are glued on the yellow dowels and white beads on blue dowels.

Slide axles through the screw eyes. In this pull toy, the red axles slide through the screw eyes on yellow block. A green bead is glued on the free ends. This is repeated with yellow axles on the blue block and blue axles on the red block.

Glue movable eyes on the front of the block or paint eyes. Set aside to dry.

When glue is dry, attach a small screw eye to both ends of the two blocks and one end of the third block. This allows you to hook cars together. Gently spread apart the screw eyes. Do this before screwing into the wood or you could split the wood. Center the screw eyes about 1/8 inch up from the bottom of the blocks. A pilot hole is not needed because these are small-shanked screw eyes.

Use pliers to gently squeeze the screw eyes closed. Tie the red bead on one end of the cord or thong. Tie the other end of the cord or thong to the screw eye in the front of the yellow block.

Eye-Catching Mobiles

Mobiles provide early visual stimulation for a baby. They are also an inexpensive way to decorate baby's environment. A few projects in this section, such as the *T-Shirt Mobile*, page 124, or *Photo Mobile*, page 117, add or change elements as time passes, contributing to a child's memory development.

Mobiles in this section are for looking at, not handling. If they are pulled, they will fall apart or become unbalanced. This ruins your efforts and the baby's enjoyment of the project. If the mobile is placed low enough to be reached, such as above the crib, the child could be hurt by falling pieces or things he'll put in his mouth.

For hanging projects baby can touch, see the *Three-Kittens Crib Toy*, page 91, or the *Crib Exerciser*, page 99.

HANGING MOBILES

There's a trick to hanging a mobile—you have to balance all the parts. To achieve balance, the elements must be hung one at a time. Always work from opposite sides.

The *Shower Mobile*, page 115, *Fabric Butterflies*, page 116, *Photo Mobile*, page 117, and *Sea Mobile*, page 118, are all hung from rings. Small rings extend to a larger element from which the mobile is hung. With the butterflies and sea creatures, the larger element is a wood or brass ring. On the *Shower Mobile*, it's a paper-plate holder. The *Photo Mobile* uses a straw wreath. Regardless of what the second hanging element is, all mobiles hang from a ring the same way.

For example, to hang the butterflies on the *Fabric Butterflies*, begin with the butterfly that will be on top. Tie a single piece of clear fishing line around its upper body with a double knot. Cut the fishing line long enough to extend from the body to the large ring. The string is wrapped once or twice around the top ring and held with a double knot.

Always work from opposite sides of the larger ring. The next element to be hung and balanced is the fourth butterfly. Before cutting the line, estimate the length needed to extend from the butterfly to the larger, then smaller ring. Attach the butterfly the same way as the first. Keep the larger ring horizontal.

The third butterfly to be attached hangs second from the top. It is secured to a third point on the larger ring, exactly between the first two. The line holding the fifth butterfly is hung opposite the third butterfly. The second and sixth butterflies are attached opposite one another.

During the attachment process, continue balancing one element against the other. Keep the center ring horizontal and even.

Children's Embroidery-Hoop Projects

Characters like these can be grouped together or hung separately, as mobiles or wall hangings. The kitty and bunny are drawn with fabric markers, page 20. The abstract "shoot-out" scene is a felt collage made from scraps. The bunny and duck are traced from cookie cutters.

The duck is sewn on burlap with a running-stitch, see page 9. Other felt pieces are glued in position. See page 13 for information on gluing.

Shower Mobile

This party decoration is a nice addition to a nursery. Fill baskets with trinkets and artificial flowers. These items can be found in stores selling party and craft supplies. Hang the flowers and trinkets with curling ribbon from a paper-plate holder. See page 114 for more information on hanging mobiles. Also see page 127 for a Shower Wreath.

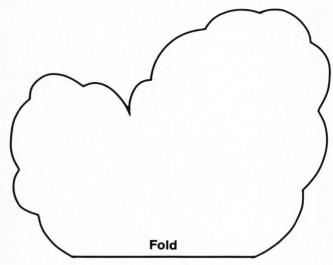

Fold

Figure A—This design is traced, then cut out. Or do free-hand cutting, creating design as you cut.

Fabric Butterflies

This can be a team project. A child can help make the butterflies and an adult can hang them. Baby will respond to the movement and bright, translucent colors of the fabric.

EQUIPMENT
- Scissors, page 20
- Pinking shears, page 20
- Felt-tip pens, page 20

MATERIALS
- 6 wood, slip-on clothespins
- Spray paint
- Pieces of organdy or other thin fabric, in many shades or colors to make wings
- 6 colored pipe cleaners
- 3 yards of fishing line or nylon thread for hanging
- 1 brass or wood ring, 3 inches in diameter
- 1 brass or wood ring, 9 inches in diameter

MAKING BUTTERFLIES
If you plan to paint clothespins, do it at this point. Let paint dry thoroughly before attaching wings.

Wings can be made in different patterns. For the top wing of a 4-inch clothespin, cut a fabric rectangle 8x5''. Fold it in half across its width. Instead of using fabric, you can use tissue paper. Tissue paper is easy for a child to work with, and the mobile is as pretty.

Trace the pattern piece shown in Figure A and cut out. When you are finished cutting, open wings out. In the middle of the top side of the wing, apply a few drops of glue. This will hold the fabric in place against the inside of the clothespin. Gently slide the fabric wing in the clothespin, pushing it into gathers. Press the part with the glue against the inside top. For the bottom wing, repeat this process, gluing fabric to the clothespin on the inside bottom.

Twist pipe cleaners around the head of each clothespin for antennae. For hanging mobiles from rings, see page 114.

116

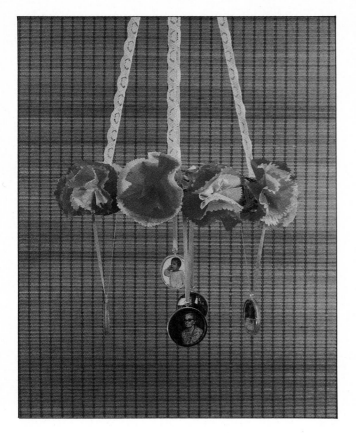

MAKING MOBILE

If the baby is not yet born or if you can't get photos, use cutouts from magazines, gift-wrap or other sources. Consider filling the center frame with a photo of mom during the pregnancy. Leave others empty for her to fill when baby is born.

Fit pictures into frames. Buy or make flowers, and arrange them in order around the wreath. Secure each flower in place by wrapping the wire stem around the wreath and around the top of the stem.

Cut the trim into three 1-5/8-yard sections. Wrap each piece of trim around 1/3 of the wreath. Ends leading to the ring are left on the outside. Secure them with straight pins. See Figure A.

Cut a 1-3/4-inch piece of ribbon. Thread the end through the center of the craft frame. Stitch ribbon ends together over the craft ring. Fold the ends of the trim over the ring. Balance the wreath so it hangs 4 to 5 inches above the craft frame hanging from the center. See page 114 for information on hanging a mobile.

After it's balanced, stitch trim and ribbon in place under the ring. Hang the wreath. Cut the remaining ribbon into four 7/8-yard pieces. Thread the ribbon through the rings of the craft frames. Tie each ribbon around the wreath, an equal distance from the last one, at the same level.

Photo Mobile

This mobile will add a festive touch to a room. It is also an educational tool for teaching baby to recognize and name things. With the baby at the center, include pictures of family members, friends, pets and even a stuffed doll or toy. As the child gets older, she may want to fill the frames with pictures of her own.

EQUIPMENT
- Scissors, page 20

MATERIALS
- 1 straw wreath, 12 inches or smaller. Straw may shed, so don't hang it above baby's sleeping area. You may also use a Styrofoam ring and wrap it with crepe paper.
- Tissue paper for flowers
Or
- Silk, plastic or other artificial flowers
- 1 piece of floral wire, 10 inches long, for each flower
- 1 craft ring, 2 inches in diameter
- 4-7/8 yards lace or other trim
- 5-1/4 yards of 1/4-inch-wide ribbon
- 5 craft frames
- 10 photos

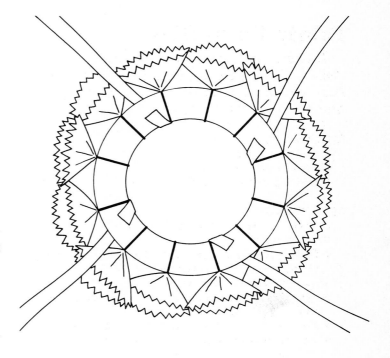

Figure A—The wreath in the photo is hung with three strands of lace. You can use four strands. Divide sections in quarters, instead of thirds.

Sea Mobile

This mobile adds bright color to the nursery. The colorful felt creatures will capture baby's attention.

EQUIPMENT
- Embroidery needle, page 20
- Straight pin, page 20
- Push pin, page 20
- Paper for patterns
- Pencil with eraser
- Pen
- Ruler, page 20
- Tool for stuffing, page 18

MATERIALS
- Scraps of felt in colors shown or as desired. A 9x12'' piece of felt is large enough for three figures.
- Small amount of six-strand embroidery thread in desired colors
- 3-1/3 yards ribbon in desired pattern and color
- 1 plastic or wood ring, 7 inches long
- 1 plastic or brass ring, 1-1/4 inches long
- 14 yards acrylic yarn
- Less than 1 bag of polyfill
- White glue

TRACING AND CUTTING
Trace patterns on the felt scraps with a pen. Place the traced felt over another piece in the same color. Cut both pieces at the same time. When stitching the pieces together, reverse the order so ink is on the inside. Continue until all patterns are traced and cut.

SEWING AND STUFFING
Divide the six-strand embroidery thread into two three-strand pieces. Knot one strand, and set the other strand aside for another figure.

Use the needle as a balance. Insert it part-way into the felt to see how you want the figure to hang. If you want the fish to hang level, insert the needle near the top of the fin. If you want it to swim downward, insert the needle near the back fin. See Figures B, C and D on page 120. This procedure does not apply to the *turtle* or *starfish*. See below for special instructions.

Make the first stitch on the inside of the felt pieces, so the knot is hidden. Use the buttonhole-stitch, page 10, and continue stitching. Stuff the figure as you go along.

When you are about 1/2 inch from the end, check the length of thread on the needle. If several inches are left, finish stitching. Use the excess to hang the figure on the ring in a later step. If there is not enough thread, tie a knot on the inside. Cut the thread and thread the needle with a longer piece. Make your first stitch on the inside so the knot is hidden, and finish stitching the figure.

The *starfish* is not attached to the large ring with excess embroidery thread. It is attached directly to the small ring by ribbon. For the starfish, start the buttonhole-stitch at any point. When you finish sewing, cut off excess thread.

The *turtle* is tied from the large ring with excess thread. It is not balanced until after it is sewn with the buttonhole-stitch. Begin the first stitch at any point. Continue with the sewing and stuffing procedure as described for the fish.

When the figure is complete, push the needle inside as if taking one more stitch. Bring the needle out as near as possible to the top middle of the shell. If you don't want the turtle to hang parallel to other figures, bring the needle out at some other point.

Figure A—Trace patterns on felt with fabric markers.

Figure A

119

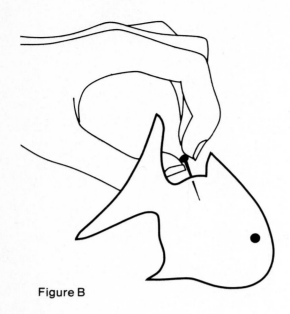

Figure B

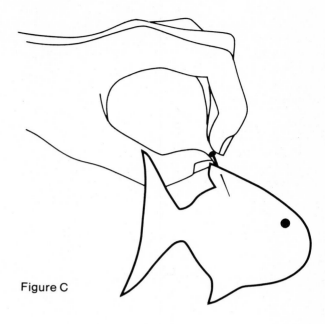

Figure C

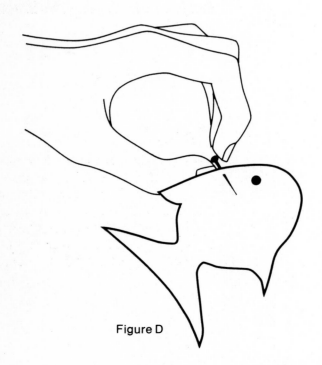

Figure D

MAKING FEATURES

Using three strands of embroidery thread, thread the needle, but don't knot thread. Make an eye with a satin-stitch, page 11. When the eye is complete, push the needle through the animal to the other side. Make the second eye.

When the second eye matches the first, begin your final stitching. Push the needle at least 1/2 inch in any direction toward a seam. Pull the needle through the felt and snip the thread.

For markings on the large fish, use a satin-stitch. Continue moving from one side to the next.

WRAPPING RING

Cut yarn into a 14-yard length and double it. To start, place the looped end over the ring. Pull the entire length through the center. See Figure E. Using two strands at once, wrap it around the ring. When you have wrapped the ring, glue ends neatly in place with white glue.

ATTACHING RIBBON

Cut the ribbon into four equal pieces. To make loops, measure 2 inches down each piece. Fold the ribbon over the 1-1/4-inch ring. Tuck 1/4 inch of the raw edge under so it's hidden. Sew the loop with several stitches.

After ribbons are sewn to the small ring, hang the ring from a doorway with a pin. Determine the desired length of the ribbons. Tie three of them an equal distance apart on the 7-inch ring. Use a single knot until the ring is balanced, then secure each with a double knot. Snip off excess ribbon. The fourth ribbon is not tied to the large ring. It hangs suspended from the center with the starfish sewn to the end of it. Sew the starfish to the ribbon with a running-stitch or other stitch, page 11.

ATTACHING ANIMALS

Tie each figure to the large ring with a single knot. Arrange figures according to weight and color. When the animals are attached and the ring is balanced, tie each ribbon with a double knot.

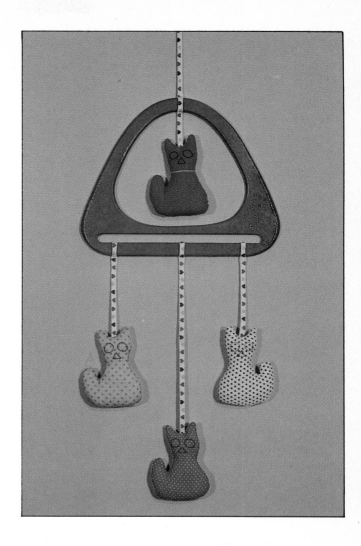

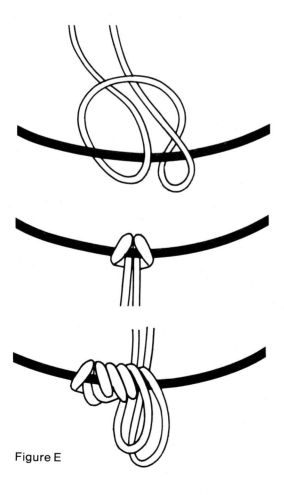

Figure E

Cat Mobile

Attach cats or other characters to a sanded, spray-painted handbag handle with shoelaces, ribbons, yarn or string. Instructions for making the cats are found with the Three-Kitten Crib Toy, page 91. Sew ties in the seams at the head instead of the sides. For another nursery project using handbag handles, see the Nursery Laundry Bag, page 47.

MAKING FACE

Design your face before decorating spools. The size of your pot will dictate proportions. The front and back sides must be equal in the weight they carry. See Figure A.

Decorate spools on both sides before gluing them together. To cover the inner sides, lay the spool flat on the felt. Trace the outer and inner circles. When cutting outer and inner circles, cut inside the lines to make the shape small enough to fit inside the spool. Glue in place and add trim.

When all pieces are decorated and glue has dried, prepare to adhere spools together with plastic glue. Follow directions on the package. Allow glue to dry before attaching the features for hanging.

MAKING HAT AND HAIR

Wash and dry the pot, then paint it with the spray paint. Measure the distance around the top of the brim before making hair. Double or triple this measurement. Cut a piece of tissue paper this length. If you need extra length, tape pieces together. Cut tissue as wide as you want. When the strip is cut, fold one long side 1/2 inch to form a rim, then fold over another 1/2 inch.

Fringe the tissue paper below this rim in 1/4-inch strips. Gather the paper at the rim with a needle and thread the way you gather a piece of fabric. Be careful not to rip the paper.

Set the gathered strip aside. The mobile must be put together before hair is glued to the hat.

Recycled Clown

Baby will love this smiling face. You can use a plant pot and any extra spools you might have. The spools used here are discarded typewriter-ribbon spools. Yours may be from adhesive tape, gift-wrap ribbon, thread or other sources.

EQUIPMENT
- Scissors, page 20
- Needle for hand-sewing, page 20
- Needle for making holes in pot, page 20
- Matches for heating needle, page 18

MATERIALS
For the face:
- Any kind of lightweight spool. Consider combining different sizes and types.
- Decorations, such as spray paint, felt, fabric, ribbon, trims, glitter, small artificial flowers

For the hat:
- Lightweight plastic pot, 7 inches in diameter
- Spray paint
- 1/2 yard of wide ribbon to tie around brim

For the hair:
- Enough tissue paper to cover the pot

For the flower:
- 3 pieces of tissue paper, 6 inches square
- 1 piece of floral wire, 12 inches long
- 1 spool of floral tape
- White glue
- Plastic model cement
- 1/2 yard of clear fishing wire

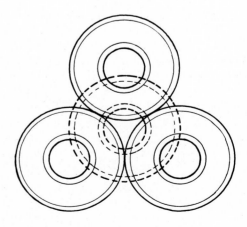

Figure A—To achieve balance, eyes must have the same weight on each side.

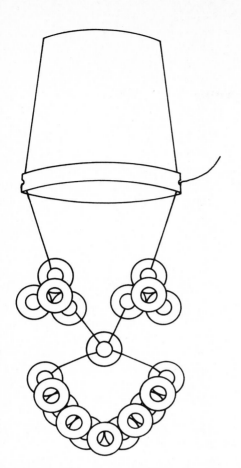

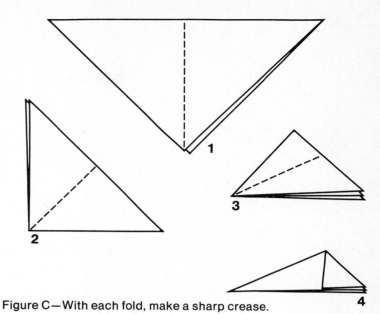

Figure C—With each fold, make a sharp crease.

Figure B—Balance pieces as you go along, so they hang evenly. Secure all ends with double knots.

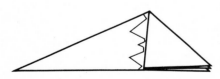

Figure D—Hold cone tightly at the point while cutting. Cut in this way or any way you like.

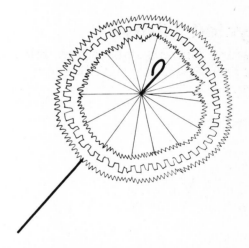

Figure E—Insert hooked wire in center of all three layers.

ASSEMBLING MOBILE

Attach the features to one another with invisible thread or fishing line. See Figure B. Heat a needle with a match. Make a hole on either side of the rim, about 1/4 inch from the inside edge. Attach the face to the pot at these two points with invisible thread. Glue hair around the outside rim of the pot, about 1/2 inch from the edge. Tie a wide ribbon or other band around the hair.

MAKING FLOWER

To make a tissue-paper flower, cut 3 squares of tissue paper. Fold each square in half diagonally, then fold in half again. Fold in half a third, then a fourth time. See Figure C. With the three cones folded, cut petals in descending heights. See Figure D.

Open the cones and stack them with the smallest on top. Straighten a piece of floral wire. Hook it at one end to keep petals from falling off. See Figure E. Gently close the tissue paper over the hooked wire. Wrap the base of the flower with wire and floral tape. To finish, add the flower to the pot by threading it into one of the water holes. Once inside, twist the wire to keep it from falling out.

T-Shirt Mobile

Recycle T-shirts to make a mobile. All you need are embroidery hoops and shoelaces. As the child outgrows them, old T-shirts can be fitted into hoops. The first mobile becomes a pair, and eventually, a group.

EQUIPMENT
- Scissors, page 20
- Needle for hand-sewing, page 20
- Safety blade

MATERIALS
- Embroidery hoops in various sizes
- Outgrown T-shirts. For every two T-shirts, you need 1 embroidery hoop.
- Fancy shoelaces, in any length. For three embroidery hoops, three shoelaces are needed.
- Ribbons, lace or other trim to fit inside hoops
- White glue

GETTING READY
Construction of this mobile is fairly easy. You must plan ahead before you begin. Think about the sizes and colors of the T-shirts. Suspended hoops are independent of one another, so there will be *two* sides of the mobile. You must determine where hoops and T-shirts will be placed.

Before cutting T-shirts to fit the hoops, you must understand the mobile is constructed from the bottom up. T-shirts in the smallest hoop are attached by a shoelace to the second hoop, and so on up the mobile. If T-shirts are cut and placed in the hoops before strings are added, there is no place to attach strings.

MAKING MOBILE
Begin with two T-shirts for the smallest hoop. Cut the parts out of the T-shirts to be set in the hoops. Leave extra fabric to trim later.

With the wrong-sides together, lay the cut T-shirts over the bottom part of the separated hoop. Center each as you want it to appear inside the ring. With the screw on top, place the

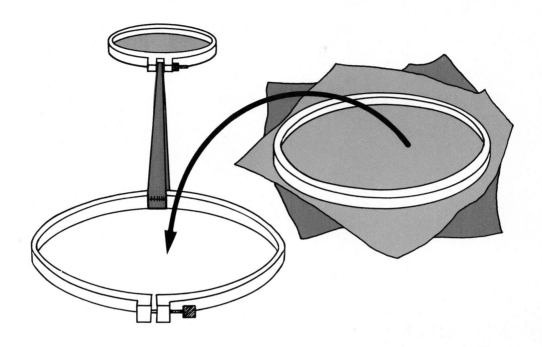

Figure A—It is necessary to align parts. Some minor adjustments can be made after hoop has been set and tightened.

top ring over the bottom ring and tighten it. Center the T-shirt by pulling each side separately. Stretch fabric tight to prevent sagging.

When T-shirts are set, trim excess fabric from the outside of the hoop. Cut as close to the edge of the hoop as possible, using a safety blade.

Determine the distance you want between each hoop. Hoops in these mobiles are 6-1/2 inches apart. Cut the shoelace to form a loop, and cut off plastic ends. Thread the shoelace through the space underneath the screw of a hoop. Join loose ends by sewing them together over the top ring of the middle hoop.

Set aside the first hoop. Prepare T-shirts for

the middle and bottom hoops the same way as the first hoop. Position the shoelace on the inside middle hoop so stitching is concealed. Align the screw and shoelace, so the mobile hangs straight. Secure the top middle hoop over the bottom hoop. See Figure A. Trim away extra fabric.

Attach another shoelace to the top of the middle hoop. Complete construction of the mobile as described above. Keeping the screw on the top of the hoop, align the hoop with the others. Finish with one last shoelace for hanging. Glue trim to the inside of the rings. See page 13 for gluing instructions.

Wall Hangings

Decorating the walls of the nursery is like getting ready for a celebration. Instead of restricting baby's world to a particular character or theme, give him collages, shadow boxes, personal cartoons, decorative appliqués and versatile wreaths to learn from and enjoy.

Shower Wreath

Items for this project can be found in stores carrying party goods or craft supplies. Wrap crepe paper around a Styrofoam wreath. Glue ends to the back with white glue. Attach artificial flowers, leaves and other trinkets to the wreath. Secure in place with decorative straight pins or glue. Around the outside, add a small frame. Make flowers from baby socks, page 144. After baby is born, a photograph replaces the framed cut-out or sticker.

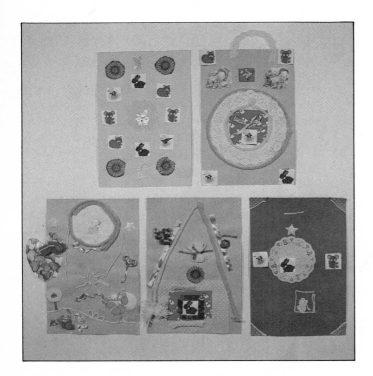

Gift-Wrap Collage

You can use many different materials for gift-wrap. This collage uses gift-wrap and ribbons from baby's shower. A group of first-grade students made the collages in this photograph to help decorate baby's nursery. See page 13 for gluing information.

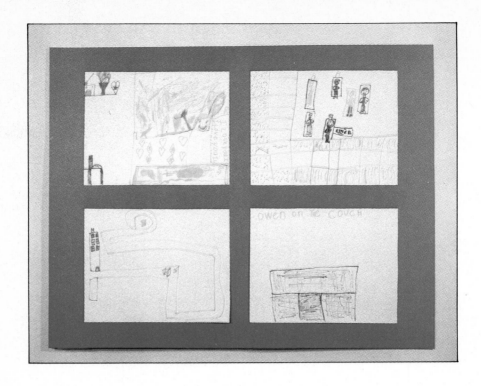

Storytelling

The story of baby's birth portrayed by cartoons is interesting when told from the viewpoint of a friend or family member. The project can be especially significant for an older brother or sister at the time of baby's birth. The event of the birth is described from his or her point of view.

When pictures are hung in the nursery, the brother or sister visibly takes part in welcoming baby. This leads to a feeling of participation and perhaps a desire to care for the baby in other ways. Artwork will be valuable when baby is old enough to appreciate the content, and the older child is reminded of the initial welcome.

EQUIPMENT
- Scissors
- Magic markers, page 20
- Colored pencils or crayons

MATERIALS
- Several sheets of paper, cut to a manageable size
- Double-side tape or white glue
- Poster board or frames large enough to hold pictures

BEGINNING ARTWORK

The trick to getting the child to start the artwork is to avoid pressure. Invite the child to draw pictures telling what he or she feels about the new baby. Don't be concerned about background or sequence.

If the child does not want to tell a story through a series of pictures, encourage him to draw one or two. The child may have trouble focusing on one aspect of the event. Refresh his or her memory with examples, such as taking mommy to the hospital or seeing the baby for the first time. Photos can help the child recall other moments or serve as models for a new interpretation.

If you want more control over the choice of subjects and number of drawings, present the child with a selection of photos. Ask him or her to recreate the scenes on paper.

For children interested in writing, suggest telling the story in words.

HANGING ARTWORK

There is more than one way to hang the completed artwork. You can arrange pictures in a logical order on cut-to-fit poster board. Adhere them with glue or sticky tape. Another way is to cut the drawing paper in sizes to fit inexpensive, standard frames. Hang cartoons in a group.

Quilted Wall Hanging

This quilt is smaller than a bed quilt but made the same way. A wall hanging brightened by premade appliqués is an ideal project for a beginner. See page 26 for Appliquéd Quilts, page 6 for bias, and page 18 for loops.

If your appliqué has a back piece, use the same fabric for single bias and loops. Stitch both ends of the loop on the back of the bias when quilting and binding are finished.

Cutlery Box

When a toddler is able to sort objects and starts collecting things, move the cutlery box or crate to a level the child can reach. Decorate with decals, ribbons, stickers or other trim. Replace dangerous or fragile items with durable toys. See page 84 for the Caterpillar Sock Toy.

Storage Hutch

Wood soda crates, plastic milk-carton crates and other decorative plastic crates can be found in variety and grocery stores. If you obtain a used plastic crate, be sure to clean it up with detergent and household cleaner before use. Sand any rough edges on wood crates.

Secure a crate above the changing table to hold diaper pins, cotton balls, toys and other things for baby. You may want to include some of the projects pictured here—Wood Blocks, page 111, Tiny Playmates, page 86, Pins in a Basket, page 146, Covered Shape Box, page 108.

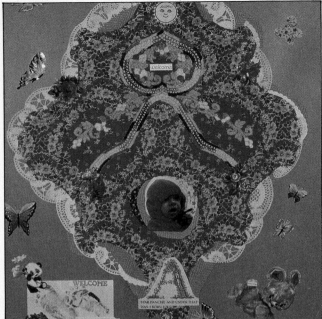

Close-up picture of part of collage.

Baby Collage in Covered Frame

A collage of baby's mementos protected behind glass can remain hanging after the infant has grown.

EQUIPMENT
- **Gluing supplies, page 13**
- **Razor blade**
- **Cutting board or thick piece of cardboard to use with the razor**

MATERIALS
- **Poster board or material stiff enough to hold the weight of glue and elements**
- **White glue**
- **Spray adhesive**
- **Elements for the collage. See Selecting Materials below.**
- **Frame**
- **Picture-hanging wire**
- **2 screw eyes**
- **Fabric to cover frame. You will need 4 inches more than the size of the frame.**

SIZE
The size can vary, but choose a backing board to fit a ready-made frame. Standard sizes for ready-made frames found in stores include 8x10", 9x12", 11x14", 16x20" and 20x24". Ready-made frames provide an allowance for the picture. If the frame is not ready-made, make backing board 1/8 inch smaller to fit in the frame.

DESIGNING COLLAGE
Place the collected items in a pleasing arrangement on the board. See Figure A. Keep a 1/4-inch margin on all sides for the frame allowance. Cutting and gluing are permanent, so wait until you have a specific idea of the picture before doing either.

SELECTING MATERIALS
Collect special materials for a baby collage. No two collages will be alike. The materials used in this collage include an embroidered neck piece and fabric from maternity shifts, scraps of fabric, parts of cards and letters, decals, a photo of the baby, hospital footprints and an identification bracelet.

You may not want to glue items such as the baby's footprints to a permanent collage. Use materials such as the birth announcement or an invitation to the baby shower, baby gift-wrap and cutouts from magazines and other sources. If you don't have a picture of the baby, cut out pictures of other babies or baby animals. Also see *Gift-Wrap Collage,* page 127.

Cardboard comes in several thicknesses. Use thicker cardboard if the elements in the collage are heavy. Canvas or hardboard can also be used. These heavier backings will not warp. In this collage, poster board was used for its color, but hardboard painted blue could have been used. You may prefer a white background, or you may cover the background with fabric.

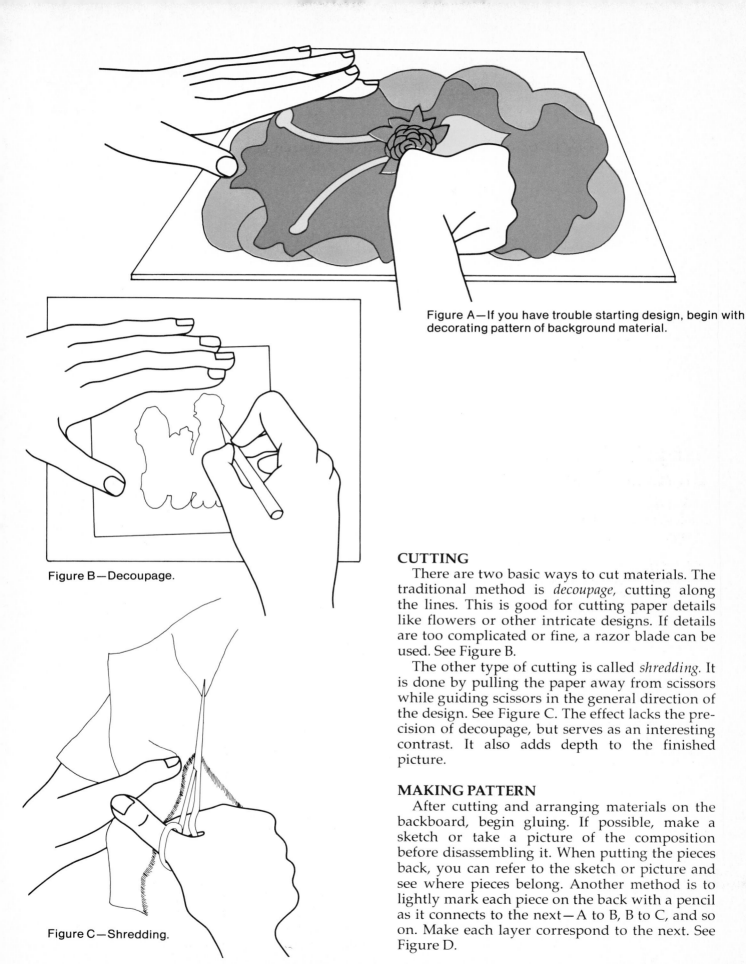

Figure A—If you have trouble starting design, begin with decorating pattern of background material.

Figure B—Decoupage.

Figure C—Shredding.

CUTTING

There are two basic ways to cut materials. The traditional method is *decoupage*, cutting along the lines. This is good for cutting paper details like flowers or other intricate designs. If details are too complicated or fine, a razor blade can be used. See Figure B.

The other type of cutting is called *shredding*. It is done by pulling the paper away from scissors while guiding scissors in the general direction of the design. See Figure C. The effect lacks the precision of decoupage, but serves as an interesting contrast. It also adds depth to the finished picture.

MAKING PATTERN

After cutting and arranging materials on the backboard, begin gluing. If possible, make a sketch or take a picture of the composition before disassembling it. When putting the pieces back, you can refer to the sketch or picture and see where pieces belong. Another method is to lightly mark each piece on the back with a pencil as it connects to the next—A to B, B to C, and so on. Make each layer correspond to the next. See Figure D.

GLUING

Read the information or gluing on page 13, then follow directions on the can. Spray the adhesive on the backs of larger pieces. Allow glue to get tacky before applying pieces to the board. Apply all-purpose glue with a toothpick for smaller pieces. If necessary, these pieces can be held with tweezers. The glass helps hold pieces in place, so use glue sparingly.

COVERING FRAME

You need an inexpensive frame to fit the backing board. Fabric to cover the frame should be 4 inches wider and longer than the frame. If the frame is 8x10″, you will need a 12x14″ piece of fabric.

Remove the glass from the frame, and set it aside. Spread newspaper over the work area. Lay the frame face up and spray it with a coat of spray adhesive. Turn the frame over and carefully place it face down on the fabric. Let glue dry a bit, then spray the back of the frame and the outer and inner edges.

When glue gets tacky, fold the top edge of the fabric over the side of the frame. Press fabric firmly along the outer edge and back of the frame. Smooth out wrinkles as you press the corner. Work around the frame until fabric is secured to the back. When glue has dried, trim excess fabric that hangs over edges.

Leaving the frame face down, cut a piece out of the fabric that covers the frame opening. Cut this piece 2 inches smaller than the frame opening. This allows for 2 inches of fabric to fold to the inside. When the inside piece is cut, remove it and set it aside. Make a diagonal cut in each corner from inside the edge of the frame to the outer edge of the fabric. See Figure E.

With the frame face down, spray the wrongside of the fabric with glue. Pull the fabric at each side up and over the back of the frame. While smoothing, press fabric securely to the back and inner edge of the frame. Allow glue to dry. Trim excess fabric and replace the glass. Your collage is ready for framing. See page 13 for attaching wire.

Figure D—Move completely around picture until all items are labeled and positioned on pattern.

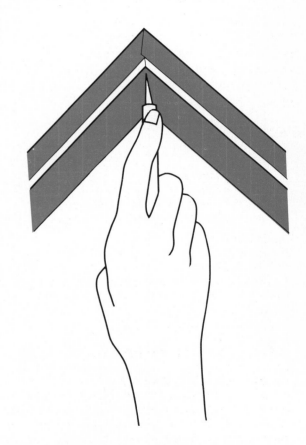

Figure E—Make a diagonal cut in each corner.

Shadow-Box Birth Announcement

A shadow box lets you announce the baby's birth and display mementos that are often packed away. This shadow box is made from a tool drawer, but you can use anything from a wood cutlery box or desk sorter to a premade, purchased shadow box.

EQUIPMENT
- **Ruler or other measuring device, page 20**
- **Pencil**
- **Scissors, page 20**
- **Hand-sewing needle, page 20**
- **Materials for cross-stitch, see page 10**
- **Patterns for the alphabet and numbers**

MATERIALS
For the box:
- **Any size box**
- **Objects to display, such as umbilical-cord clamp, pacifier, spoons, shoes, hospital band, footprints**
- **Double-sided tape**
- **White glue**
- **1 spool of invisible nylon thread**

For the inserts:
Inserts are backings made to fit in some sections of the box. They can be set against the back of the box or brought forward, giving the box color and dimension. They help bring smaller mementos forward to display them better.
- **1 sheet of cardboard or mat board**
- **A few handfuls of polyfill, page 18**
- **Fabric to cover each insert**
- **Blocks of foamcore, sponge or cardboard tube to put behind inserts to keep them in position**

For the blocks:
- **A few household sponges. If they are flat, glue 2 or 3 together to form the desired height.**
- **Small amounts of fabric to cover blocks**

ATTACHING ITEMS

Items are attached to inserts after inserts have been secured in sections of the box. Inserts are cut the same size as the section. Behind each insert is placed foamcore, sponge or cardboard tube. Mementos, such as umbilical-cord clamps, pacifiers and spoons, are kept in place with invisible nylon thread.

Use double-sided tape to secure shoes, footprints and hospital bands. Don't use glue except when adding decorative touches, such as the bottle or bunny.

Figure A—Cut board to measurements of inside edges of box and filler the size of board. Fabric is cut 1/2 inch larger on all sides so it can be pulled over and glued to board. See page 150 for covering frames and backboards.

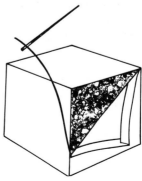

Figure B—Cut blocks in desired size from sponges. Cut fabric squares 1/4 inch larger on all sides than size of block. Iron hem allowance on wrong-side of fabric on each square. Sew squares together around block with embroidery-stitches, page 9.

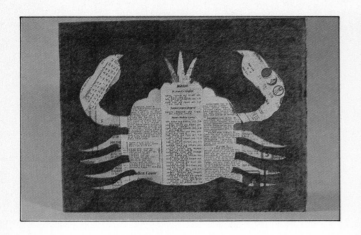

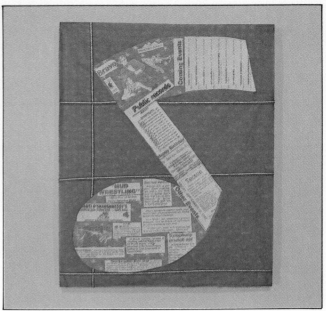

News-Clipping Collage

A newsprint collage marks details of baby's birthday. A stencil of the astrological sign or other symbol frames the announcement found in public records and other clippings.

EQUIPMENT
- **Enlarging supplies, page 12**
- **Paper for pattern**
- **Pencil with eraser**
- **Ruler, page 20**
- **Scissors and razor blade, page 20**
- **Cutting board or thick piece of cardboard**
- **Gluing supplies, page 13**

MATERIALS
- **Plastic-box frame. These collages are 8x10'' and 9x11''. You can make yours any size.**
- **Or**
- **Flat piece of cardboard to be slipped into ready-made frame.**
- **Clippings. Two newspapers are needed—one printed on the day of baby's birth and one announcing baby's birth. Except for the announcement, all clippings come from paper printed on the day of birth.**
- **White glue**

ENLARGING PATTERN
Enlarge the pattern for the note or astrological sign, using the technique described on page 12. Cut out the piece according to the patterns shown in Figures A or B.

MAKING STENCIL
Trace a pattern in the center of the paper to serve as the background. If the frame is 8x10'', the background is the same. Make a stencil by cutting out the pattern with a blade. Discard the center piece.

COVERING BACKGROUND
If you use the plastic cover, cover the sides and background. They can be contrasted with reversible-pattern rice paper or two kinds of gift-wrap. If you use flat cardboard, only the solid color is needed. Consider using construction paper, in addition to rice paper or gift-wrap.

If using a box with a plastic frame, remove the frame. Wrap the front and sides with patterned paper. The stencil and clippings cover the front, but the pattern is visible on all four sides. This serves as a frame. See Figure C. If using flat cardboard, use the same method, but cover only the front.

Figure A   Each square equals 1 inch.

Figure B
Each square equals 1 inch.

DESIGNING PICTURE

The theme can vary from one announcement to the next. An announcement might focus on political views, or it might include a weather report and astrological forecast. Other possibilities include headlines about fashion, movie schedules and want ads.

Center the stencil on top of the flat cardboard or wrapped box. With the stencil in place, trace the appropriate astrological sign on the background so the shape is visible when pieces are glued. Arrange clippings under the stencil. See Figure D. Use tweezers for placement of smaller pieces.

When the design is complete, make a quick sketch of the arrangement of the clippings. This will help you remember where everything goes. Disassemble the clippings before gluing.

GLUING

With a gluing tool, see page 13, apply a little glue to the top corners of the box. Tack the top corners of the stencil in place. Smooth the corners as you work. If too much of the stencil is glued, there won't be enough room for the clippings underneath.

When glue dries, lay the stencil back without creasing it. Apply a little glue evenly to the back of each clipping, page 13. The glass or plastic will hold pieces in place, so not much glue is needed.

When clippings are glued in place, tack down the bottom corners of the stencil. If using a box, you are ready for the plastic cover. If using flat cardboard, you are ready for framing.

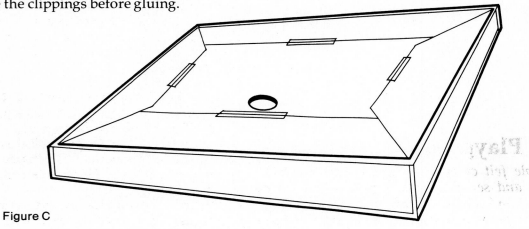

Figure C

Figure D—Do not glue clippings until design is complete.

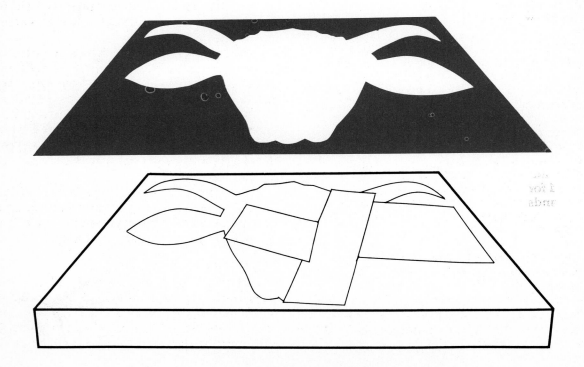

Felt Playground

Simple felt cutouts are glued to a felt background and set against burlap. Cutouts can be mounted on heavy cardboard and put in a ready-made frame or mounted on hardboard. The size of this playground is 20x24''.

EQUIPMENT
- Gluing supplies, page 13
- Embroidery supplies

MATERIALS
- Less than 1 sheet each of various colors of felt
- 1 piece of brown felt for tree, 9x12''
- 2 pieces of green felt for leaves, each 8x12''
- 1 piece of blue felt for sky, 18x12''
- 1 piece of green felt for grass, 18x6''
- 1 piece of burlap, 24x28''
- Embroidery thread in desired colors for faces, boy's hair and other trim
- 54 strands or 9 six-strand groups of embroidery thread for each set of braids
- 18 strands of embroidery thread for doll's hair
- Sturdy cardboard and ready-made frame, 20x24''

Or

- 1 piece of hardboard, 20x24x1/4''
- 1 yard of picture-hanging wire
- 2 screw eyes
- White glue
- Spray adhesive
- Lace trim for girl's pinafore and doll's petticoat, optional

ENLARGING AND TRACING

Enlarge the patterns in Figure A, using the technique described on page 12. Some patterns are laid on top of one another. These overlaid patterns are indicated by dash lines. Separate the overlaid patterns by transferring them to tracing paper. Trace the boy's jumpsuit, then trace the shirt for the girl on the fence.

After patterns are separated and enlarged, cut them out. The cat pattern is in two parts. Enlarge its entire form, then enlarge its head separately. The boy's head will stand out from the background of the tree, and he will have a clearly defined face.

TRANSFERRING PATTERNS TO FELT

The patterns on page 139 make more than one piece. The same facial pattern is used for all children. The doll's face is indicated by a smaller circle inside this pattern. The same arms can be used for both girls. The hands can also be used for the boy.

By tracing both sides of the pattern, the girl's right leg can be used as her left leg. The foot attached to the leg can also be used for the boy and girl on the fence.

You will make three necks. The doll has her own neck. You will also make two shoes, nine fence posts and 20 clumps of leaves, each leaf 10 inches in size.

For the sky, the 18x12'' felt does not need to be altered. For the grass, the 18x6'' felt must be shaped into a hill. With your scissors, round the top-left corner. This will serve as a gradual slope at the top of the hill. After allowing an 8-inch length for the hill top, begin a gradual decline. Drop no more than 1 inch at the steepest point where the hill becomes level. See below for information on fringing.

Trace the patterns on the wrong-side so the ink is not seen when the picture is assembled. If the pattern is to be used again, trace it on one piece and cut two layers at a time.

FRINGING

Cut fringe on the grass and cat. On the grass, make straight, even cuts about 3/4 inch deep and 1/16 inch wide across the top. On the cat's tail, make cuts from 1/16 to 1/4 inch deep. On the body, cut no deeper than 1/16 inch.

EMBROIDERING

See page 9 for information on embroidery-stitches. Use single strands of thread for these stitches except belt loops. For belt loops, use three strands.

Running-Stitch—Use this stitch for eyelashes, eyebrows, cat's eyes and whiskers, belt loops for the girl on the fence, freckles for the faces of the boy and girl on the fence, and mouths for all figures, except the cat. Make a looser stitch for mouths so you can form smiles by tacking stitches into a smile-shape.

Satin-Stitch—Use this stitch for eyes on all figures except the cat. Satin-stitch cheeks on the girl with the doll and also on the doll.

Cross-Stitch—Use this stitch for the cat's mouth.

Chain-Stitch—Use this stitch for the boy's hair.

BRAIDING AND FINISHING TOUCHES

For each of the girls' hair, use 54 strands of thread or 9 six-strand groups. Cut them into 6-inch lengths. To make a part in the hair, tie a strand of thread in the center of the yarn with a double knot.

Divide the strands into groups of three. Begin braiding about 3/4 inch down from the center of each side. See page 7. For the girl on the fence, braids hang loose. Secure them with two or three strands thread, and tie thread in a bow. For the girl with the doll, braids are formed into loops and tied the same way.

For the doll's hair, cut 18 strands of thread into 2-inch pieces. Tie another strand in the center for a part. Tie ponytails with thread in another color and make bows. Make another bow out of the same color thread for the doll's dress.

Make belt loops for the girl on the fence with loose running-stitches. Knot the thread after each loop is complete. Draw two or three strands of thread through the belt loops, and tie them in a bow.

If you make a pinafore for the girl with the doll, use the dress pattern. Omit the sleeves. If you make a petticoat for the doll, use her skirt as a pattern.

ASSEMBLING FIGURES

Heads and limbs can be attached to the chil-dren's clothing by sewing or gluing. If sewing, use tiny stitches. If gluing, apply glue sparingly and evenly to the felt. Follow the same procedure for the doll and cat.

When the children, doll and cat are assembled, set aside the sky, grassy area, tree, 9 fence posts and 20 clumps of leaves.

GLUING

Iron any large creases out of the burlap. Spread newspaper over your work area, and lay burlap face down on top of the paper. Center the backing board face down on top of the burlap. Leave equal margins on all sides.

Spray adhesive on the fabric around the outside margin. Let the glue dry until it's tacky. Pull the fabric one side at a time firmly and evenly over the back of the board. This keeps the front smooth.

When the glue has dried, turn the backing board over so it is face up. Center the sky and grass over the burlap. With the spray adhesive, spray the back of the felt lightly and evenly, page 13. Firmly press the felt on the burlap.

Position the tree on the grass where the hill starts to slope. Apply glue to parts of the tree trunk and branches. The boy's foot is later tucked under a branch, so don't glue down the branch. Arrange leaves, alternating sizes and colors. Glue the back of each clump and press in position.

When the tree is finished, add the fence. Position the first post under the tree trunk, about 3/4 inch from the bottom of the grass. The next post is placed 1-1/4 inches from the first, 1/16 inch higher. Do this with all the posts. Rails weave in and out of the posts, so ends are underneath. This gives the illusion of continuous pieces. After the fence is positioned, glue it in place.

Glue down the cat, the boy hanging from the tree, the girl on the fence and the girl with the doll. Attach all the pieces to the felt background.

The baby's name and date of birth can be spelled out in felt.

ATTACHING WIRE

See page 13 for directions on attaching wire to hang the picture.

Figure A
Each square equals 1 inch.

Welcome-Baby Wreath

Like the Puff Quilt, page 24, the puff wreath is made from stuffed individual sections that are sewn together. These letters form the words Welcome Baby, but you can write other words. If you make the entire alphabet, you can make many messages, offering the child an early opportunity to learn to read.

EQUIPMENT
- Enlarging supplies, page 12
- Tracing supplies, page 20
- Sewing supplies
- Stuffing tool, page 18

MATERIALS
- 12 pieces of fabric, 6x12-3/4''
- 1/2 yard of 45-inch-wide backing fabric. This fabric does not show, so any scrap material can be used. Be sure the color isn't so dark it can be seen through the stuffed puff.
- 1/4 yard of 45-inch-wide fabric for letters
- Decorative trim, such as lace or ribbon
- 1 box of 1-3/4-inch T-pins
Or
- Velcro or snaps for the back of each letter
- Less than 1 bag of polyfill, page 18
- 1 Styrofoam wreath, 16 inches in diameter
- 5 to 6 inches of wire, string, ribbon or other material for hanger

MAKING WREATH SECTIONS

For visibility, the colors of the letters should contrast with the color of the background. The letters in the wreath in the photo are made from five fabrics, but any number of colors can be used. Arrange colors in the best order to lead the eye across the word. If one fabric is darker, like the purple B, use it to begin a word. This does not draw unnecessary attention to the middle of the word.

Cut 12 pieces of puff fabric, 6x12-3/4''. See Figure A. Cut 12 pieces of backing fabric, 5x11''. Place the wrong-side of the puff fabric next to the wrong-side of the backing fabric. Pin corners in place.

To make pieces fit, make an inverted pleat in the center of one end of the larger section. Make a 5-inch inverted pleat from this end on each side. Leave the other end open. Pin pleats in place so corners and raw edges match.

Machine-stitch a 1/4-inch seam around the three sides with pinned tucks. It is easiest to sew all the pillows, then turn them right-side out. Stuff them and close the openings. See Figure B.

When stuffing is complete, pin the open end closed with another tuck in the middle. Raw edges will be covered by the overlapping side of the puff. Do *not* fold them in before machine-stitching.

When puffs are stuffed and closed, arrange them around the wreath. Puffs are not sewn to one another until later. Pin each puff to the wreath with pins. Bring the ends of each puff around the wreath and pin edges together at the back. Match seams and overlap raw edges.

With a hand-stitch, sew these edges together all the way around the wreath. Tack one section to the next at two or three points. You can also sew sections together at all points with a running-stitch, page 11. This keeps sections from separating on the front of the wreath.

MAKING LETTERS AND BIRD

Both sides of the letters are the same size and are made from the same fabric. Enlarge the pattern, using the technique described on page 12. Cut out the pattern pieces according to the pattern shown in Figure C.

The letters A, B and O are not made the same way as the other letters. Other letters are easily turned right-side out after they're sewn. The letters A and B are made in two parts. Sew, stuff and close each part before sewing pieces together by hand to make each letter.

For the letter O, cut out two 12x1-1/2'' strips. Place right-sides together and sew 1/4-inch seams on three sides. Leave one of the shorter ends open. Turn the strip right-side out and stuff. Close the letter and form an O-shape. Stitch the ends closed. The seam can be concealed with a bow or other trim.

Make the bird the same way as the one-piece letters. Enlarge the pattern, using the technique described on page 12. Cut out the pattern pieces according to the pattern shown in Figure D. You can also trace a bird or other shape from a cookie cutter. The figure can be decorated in any way. This one is embroidered with a feather-stitch on the body. Eyes are done in a cross-stitch and are outlined with the back-stitch. See page 9 for embroidery stitches.

To attach letters to the wreath, use 1-3/4-inch T-pins. If you plan to eventually lower the wreath so the child can play with it, use Velcro or snaps.

If you use T-pins, sew small, square patches of felt to the back of each letter on three sides. Insert the T-pin so the head is between the felt and the letter. Sew the fourth side to hold the head of the pin in place. Another way to secure letters is to tack them in place.

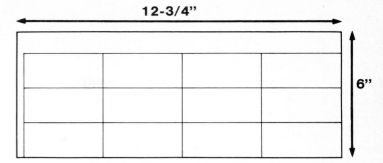

12-3/4"

6"

Figure A—For outside fabric, cut each rectangle 6x12-3/4". For backing fabric, cut each rectangle 5x11".

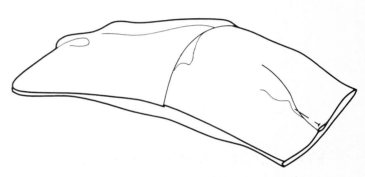

Figure B—Fill each puff with enough batting to give shape. Put more at center, where pleats are.

Figure C

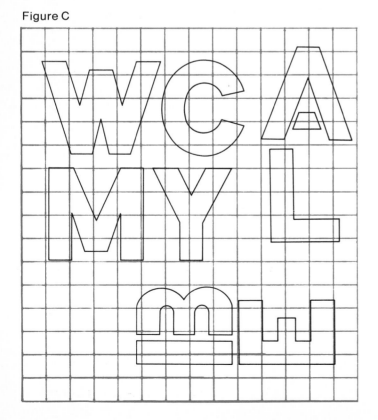

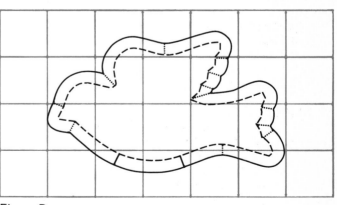

Figure D

Each square equals 1 inch.

Easy Gift Ideas

You'll find a variety of gift ideas in this section. If you want a lasting project with a personal touch, cover a purchased photo album with fabric and a covered frame. See *Covered Frames,* page 150, and *Covered Albums,* page 153. If you want to spend only a little money, use scrap fabrics to make a gift stocking. See page 155 for the *Gift Stocking.* If you want to save time, make a practical *Coupon Holder,* page 148, or decorate a *Baby's Sleeping* plaque to hang on a door, page 149. You can use the gift-wrap ideas as gifts themselves.

Gift-Wrap Ideas

These ideas make wrapping part of the gift. From left to right, the Covered Shape Box, page 108, Baby-Sock Corsage, page 144, Sticker Cartoon, below, Texture Sock, page 147 and in the middle, Pins in a Basket, page 146. The Texture Sock and the Covered Shape Box both become toys for the baby. Mom and dad will appreciate the Pins in a Basket. A Baby-Sock Corsage or Boutonniere and a homemade Sticker Cartoon are fun to give and receive.

Except for the Covered Shape Box, directions for all of the projects can be found on the following pages. For putting conventional gift-wrap to use in a collage after presents are opened, see page 127.

Framed Sticker Cartoon

Bring out the lighter side of having a baby by cartooning with stickers. The recipient may decide to slip the personal cartoons into an inexpensive frame.

EQUIPMENT
- Scissors, page 20
- 1 felt-tip pen

MATERIALS
- As many stickers as desired
- Solid-color gift-wrap
- White paper for word balloons

WRITING CAPTIONS

This group of gooney-eyed characters is attending a shower. Yours could be participating in a childbirth class or a delivery. Use several characters or only a few. Characters might represent an expectant couple exchanging comments in the labor room. Write the captions or make a game of it and invite others to fill in the empty balloons.

To attach a stem, cut a piece of wire 8 inches long. Pull out a small amount of the stuffed sock from the bottom of the flower. Wrap the wire around this base three or four times before straightening it into a stem. See Figure A.

Cut a 4- to 6-inch square of netting. Pinch it at the center to form gathers and folds. Wrap netting with wire the way the sock is wrapped, then wrap netting with floral tape. Wrap the stems of the artificial leaves.

To attach floral tape, begin at the stem base. Gently turn the stem with one hand while spiraling the tape down the wire with the other hand. See Figure B. Do not cut tape from the spool until the stem is completely covered.

Follow the same procedure when taping the flower. Add netting, leaves and any additional flowers as you go along. To keep the corsage from looking loose and disjointed, keep the items close together. Wrap tape snugly, and continue wrapping until within 1 to 2 inches of the bottom. Leave the ends of the stems to be curled with a pencil or the end of your little finger. See Figure C.

For the ribbon, wind floral tape around another piece of wire. Set the wire aside to make a ribbon of your choice or the one shown here. See Figure D. Attach the ribbon to the stem with floral wire. See Figure E.

Baby-Sock Corsage and Boutonniere

This corsage won't wilt. Flowers can be plucked and used or tucked away as a keepsake. Supplies for making corsages can be found in floral shops or craft stores. For another idea on what to do with baby-sock flowers, see the Shower Wreath, page 127.

EQUIPMENT
- Scissors, page 20

MATERIALS
- 1 pair of baby anklets, with or without lace trim on cuffs
- 2 pieces of 22/24 gage floral wire, 8 inches long
- 1 roll of green floral tape
- A few inches of floral netting
- 1 to 1-1/2 yards of 1/2-inch-wide ribbon for bow
- As many artificial leaves as desired
- 1 craft pin

MAKING CORSAGE AND BOUTONNIERE
To make the flower, turn one sock inside out. Gently stuff the heel and toe back through the center with your fingers. This shapes the top half of the cuff into a bowl. Arrange the creases of the bunched sock to define the petals of a flower.

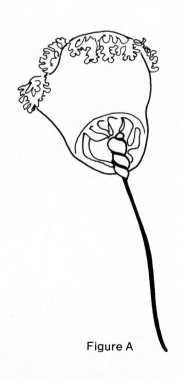

Figure A

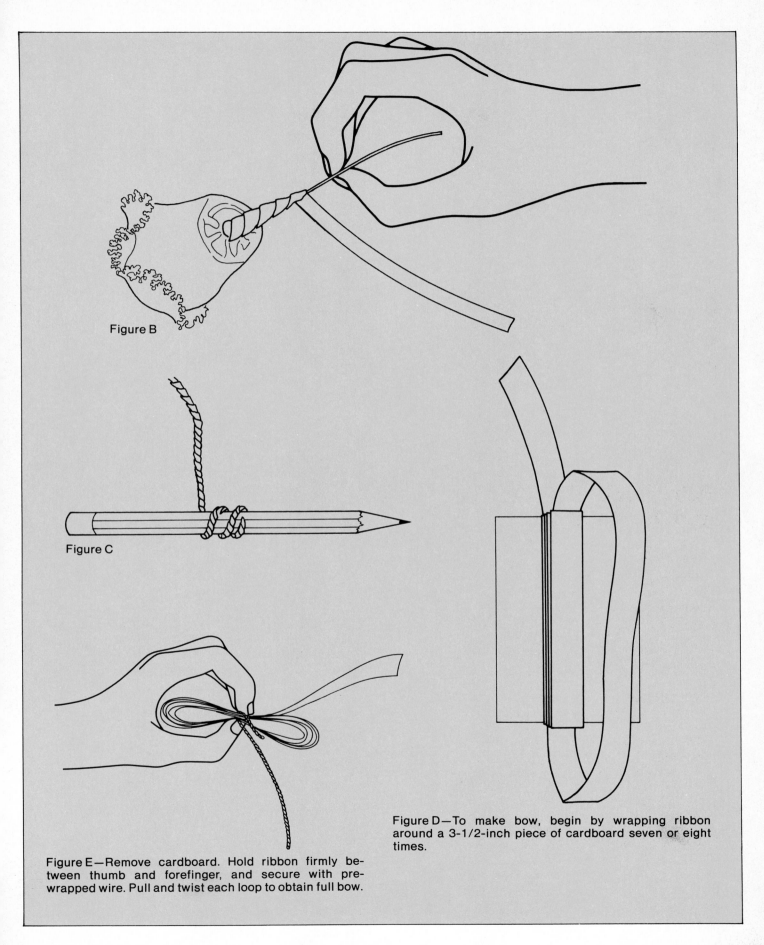

Figure B

Figure C

Figure D—To make bow, begin by wrapping ribbon around a 3-1/2-inch piece of cardboard seven or eight times.

Figure E—Remove cardboard. Hold ribbon firmly between thumb and forefinger, and secure with prewrapped wire. Pull and twist each loop to obtain full bow.

Pins in a Basket

Inexpensive baskets can be found in stores carrying craft and party supplies. They can easily be made into diaper pincushions, even if your sewing skills are limited. This practical item is a great last-minute shower gift. It can be as plain or fancy as you choose to make it.

EQUIPMENT
- **Sewing supplies**

MATERIALS
- **1 basket, any size**
- **Circle of fabric for cushion. Measure depth of basket and width. Add the width and twice the depth to get an approximate size. This gives the minimum diameter of circle needed to fill the inside of the basket.**
- **White glue**
- **Enough polyfill to fill inside of cushion**
- **Decorative lace and ribbons, optional**

ASSEMBLY

Make a circle from fabric, and cut it out. Thread your needle with a long piece of thread. Sew 1/4 inch from the raw edge all the way around with a running-stitch, page 9. Gather the fabric, page 13. When you gather the edges of the circle, you have a pouchlike piece. The opening is where the gathering thread is. Before closing the opening, firmly stuff the top with batting to form a hard cushion, page 18.

Place the cushion inside the basket. Stitch the cushion to the bottom or top at the sides with tacking-stitches. Add decorations with white glue, page 13.

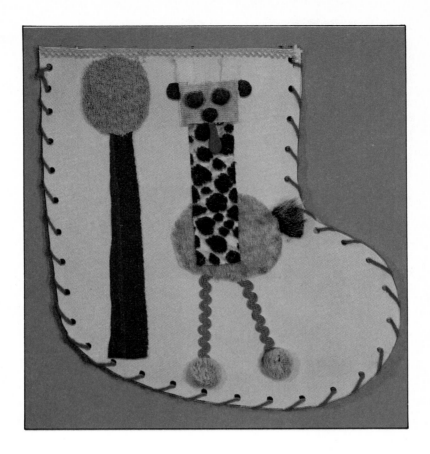

Texture Sock

Both sides of this bootie can be decorated with scraps of fabric stitched to plastic shelf liner. For a child's approach to scrap art, see the Children's Embroidery-Hoop Projects, page 115.

EQUIPMENT
- **Enlarging supplies, page 12**
- **Scissors, page 20**
- **Needle for sewing scraps on shelf liner, page 20**
- **Paper punch to prepare sock for threading yarn**

MATERIALS
- **1-1/2 yards of 12-inch-wide self-adhesive plastic shelf liner**
- **Scraps of fabrics in many textures**
- **Thread**
- **3 yards of yarn**

MAKING SOCK

Enlarge the pattern for the *Gift Stocking*, page 155, and follow construction guidelines. Trace the front of the pattern, then flip the pattern over to trace the back. Make four socks, two for the outside and two for the lining. Set aside lining pieces.

Design characters with fabric scraps. The kind of character will depend on the size and texture of the scraps. Sew pieces on the right-side of the front and back of the shelf paper. Baby will tug and chew on these things later, so use non-toxic materials and sew them securely.

When pictures are complete and top trim is added, dampen the back of each picture. Adhere to lining pieces, hiding the stitches. To keep layers from separating, tack the lining to the outside of the sock at two or three points on the rim of each cuff.

Put the sock together, with right-sides out. Punch holes 1 inch apart through all four layers around the outside edges, except the opening. Weave with yarn, knotting it at the beginning and end.

Coupon Holder

Looking for a thrifty gift idea? Clip several coupons for baby-related products. Present them with homemade offers in a simple, prequilted holder such as this one.

EQUIPMENT
- Scissors, page 20
- Needle for embroidery or hand-sewing, page 20

MATERIALS
For the holder:
- 1 piece of prequilted double-side fabric, 7-1/2x6-1/2''

Or
- Quilt layers of your own
- 1 yard of double-bias tape or homemade bias, page 6
- 1 piece of clear plastic for pockets, 7x6-1/2''
- Embroidery thread to match fabric and binding

For the coupons:
- Commercial coupons
- Construction paper for homemade offers
- Dry transfer type

Or
- Cut-out, bold-face captions from coupons to glue in new arrangement

MAKING COUPON HOLDER
Cut quilted fabric to the desired size. Fold material in half to determine the size of the pockets. Pockets on the coupon holder shown here are 3-1/2x6-1/2''. Cut plastic for the pockets to the correct size.

With medium-size stitches, baste the pockets on three sides. Cover basting and raw edges with bias binding or tape, page 6. Finish the holder with a decorative chain-stitch, page 10.

Make coupons for the parents-to-be and include them in the holder. You might give a few hours of babysitting, help at feeding time or a casserole dinner for the family. Coupons can be redeemed as needed or desired.

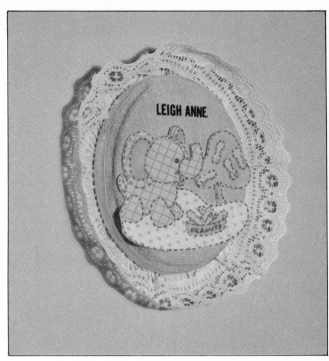

Wood Plaques and Light-Switch Covers

Here are some ways to decorate light-switch covers and wood plaques for a nursery. The name plaque is covered with fabric. Fabric is tightly pulled over the top and sides, then glued in place. See Covered Frames, page 150. Lace is glued to the fabric, and raw edges are concealed by ribbon. Lettering is done with dry-letter transfers.

The elephant scene at top is cut from another fabric. To give the appliqué body, glue it on felt cut in the same shape. The bunny and bear on the light switch are also covered with fabric.

The Baby's Sleeping sign is two wood plates, spray painted and glued together. The plaque is tied with thin velvet ribbon and decorated with stickers. Lettering is done with dry transfers found in stores carrying craft and art supplies.

Covered Frames

Here are two approaches for covering frames for baby pictures. One way is to trim frames with leftover fabric pieces from the outfit baby is wearing in the picture. The design depends on how much material you have left. Even a small amount can bring out colors in the picture.

Another way is to choose a theme from the picture you are framing and make appliqués. Place these on the picture frame. Make your own design or trace them from other sources. See page 5 for information on appliqués.

EQUIPMENT
- Felt-tip pen, page 20
- Pen or pencil
- Scissors, page 20
- Gluing supplies, page 13

MATERIALS
- Mat board in desired size for frame
- Batting to cover mat board. The amount depends of the size of the board. See page 18 for information on batting.
- Fabric 1 inch larger than mat on all sides
- Fusible interfacing to cover back of fabric. The amount depends of the size of the mat board.
- 2 pieces of 1-ply cardboard the same size as mat board
- Fabric to cover one side of one piece of cardboard. This piece must be 1 inch larger than the mat on all sides.
- Lace, ribbon or appliqués, optional

PREPARING MAT

Use the mat-board frame as a pattern. Trace the outer and inner shapes on the batting with a felt-tip pen. Cut the batting. Lightly spray glue over the top of the mat board, then gently press batting on the sprayed area.

Cut fabric 1/2 inch larger than the mat on the outside edges. Follow directions on the package, and iron fusible interfacing on the wrong-side of the cut fabric.

Lightly spray the batting-side of the mat board. Allow glue to get sticky before pressing the mat face-down on the wrong-side of the fabric.

CUTTING

After the fabric is attached to the mat board, trace around the frame opening. Angle the pen or pencil so the traced line is 1/8 inch from the edge. Trace a second line 1/2 inch inside the first line. Cut away the shape on this second line.

If working with a square or rectangle, make one cut in each corner. If working with a curved line, such as an oval, clip the curves. End 1/8 inch from the first traced line. See Figure A.

GLUING OPENING EDGES

Spread glue around the inside edges of the opening, working slowly. At opposite sides of the board, pull the fabric tightly over the board. Press the fabric into the glue. Continue around the opening until all edges are glued. Smooth the fabric and check the front side for wrinkles. Allow glue to dry.

GLUING OUTSIDE EDGES

For square or rectangular frames, glue opposite sides of the mat board along the edges. Pull

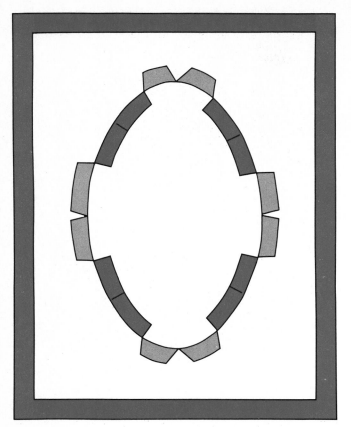

Figure A

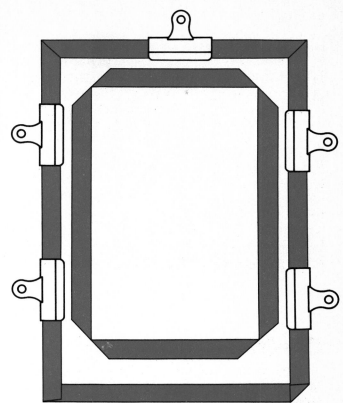

Figure B

fabric over the board and press it into the glue. Miter corners by folding a double layer of fabric to make a right angle. See Figure B. Also see page 14 for information on mitering. When mitering corners, leave 1/16 inch between the edge of the fold and the mat board. Glue end edges of the mat and pull fabric over to the wrong-side. Press into glue, then secure edges with clamps. Wait until glue has dried before adding trim.

COVERING BACKBOARD

Iron fusible interfacing to the wrong-side of the backboard fabric. Spray glue on one side of the cardboard. Lightly spray glue on the interfacing side of fabric. Allow glue to dry. Pull edges over the mat the same way the edges are pulled over the outside of the frame. See Figure B. Clamp edges or lay a heavy book over the board. If you use books, protect them by laying paper between the frame section and the book. Allow glue to dry.

ADDING TRIM

Trim is added at this point. This is before the uncovered cardboard, the covered cardboard and mat are glued together.

If you want to add lace, gather lace first. Lace should be 1 inch longer than the measurement of the opening. For inside lace trim, glue the mat around the inside edges of the wrong-side.

Arrange the lace so the wrong-side is the side that is glued. Gently lay the right-side of the lace on the right-side of the frame. Press the edges of the lace in position on the back. Allow glue to dry, right-side up, with clamps or heavy books on top of the frame.

If inside lace doesn't lay flat or flaps because of its size, tack it to the frame.

For diagonal corner trim, apply glue sparingly to the back of the trim. Press the trim in place. Pull the ends to the back of the board. Secure with more glue if necessary.

For lace trim around the outer edges of the

frame, such as on the birth announcement, page 153, turn the mat to the back and glue the outside edges. Press the edges of the right-side of the lace in the glue.

For appliqués, see page 5. Stitch them directly on the frame after it has been covered and glue has dried.

PUTTING BACKS AND FRONTS TOGETHER

Begin by gluing the back of the covered cardboard to the plain cardboard. Allow glue to dry with books piled on top of the cardboard.

To glue the frames for the photos, glue three sides of the cloth-covered cardboard on the right-side. Leave one end open so the photo can be slipped in and out. Lay the back of the covered frame on top of the glued area. Allow the glue to dry with clamps or books holding it in place. See Figure B.

Frames are also used on the *Covered Albums*, page 153, for the cross-stitch birth announcement. Glue the back of the frame to the cardboard on all sides. Glue the cardboard in the center of the frame. Lay the mounted cross-stitch on top of it. Allow glue to dry with books piled on top of the cardboard to hold it in place.

MAKING STAND

If the picture needs a stand, make your own. See Figure C. Cut two pieces the same size from the cardboard or poster board. Cut a piece of fabric 2 inches long, the width of the small end of the stand. Cut a second piece of fabric 1 inch wide and 3 inches long.

Sandwich 1/2 inch of the fabric strip between the two boards at the small end. Glue the two boards together. Glue 1/2 inch of the 3-inch strip to the lower portion of board. Glue the fabric to the cardboard on the back of the picture. See Figure D.

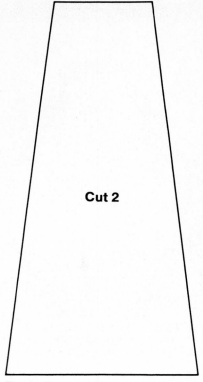

Cut 2

Figure C

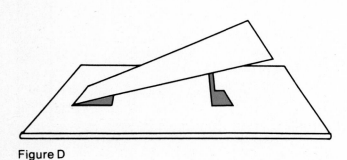

Figure D

Figure E—Musical pattern.

Each square equals 1 inch.

If baby hasn't yet arrived or photo is unavailable, leave space blank. You can also slip in a photo of the expectant parents. This photo frame is dressed-up with lace.

Fill frame of covered album with birth announcement. See page 10 for patterns and instructions on cross-stitch and for mounting cross-stitch pieces with batting.

Covered Albums

This can be a photo album, scrapbook or diary of baby's development for parents to keep. A covered album with a framed picture or birth announcement can be a personal, lasting gift for grandparents. Add decorative appliqués if you want.

EQUIPMENT
- Pen, pencil or fabric marker, page 20
- Iron
- Clothespins or other clamps to hold fabric
- Scissors
- Utility knife or straight-edge blade
- Gluing supplies, page 13

MATERIALS
- 1 3-ring, cloth-covered notebook or photo album
- 2 pieces of one-ply cardboard to fit the inside cover of notebook
- 1/2 yard of 45-inch-wide fabric for outside cover
- 1/2 yard of 45-inch-wide fabric for inside cover
- 1/2 yard fusible interfacing
- 1/2 yard of 3-ounce batting
- White glue
- Spray adhesive
- 1-1/2 yards lace, optional

PREPARING MATERIALS

Lay the album open on top of a piece of interfacing. Trace around the album, adding 1-1/2 to 2 inches to all the edges. Cut fabric the same size as the interfacing. Iron interfacing to the wrong-side of the fabric. Some chemically treated fabrics will not adhere to fusible interfacing. If this happens with your fabric, lightly spray interfacing with spray adhesive instead of ironing it. If spray adhesive is applied too heavily, the outside fabric might be stained.

Lay the album open on a piece of batting. Trace around it so the batting is the same size as the album. Cut batting along the tracing line.

Measure the inside cover of the album before cutting cardboard. One long edge of each cardboard piece will slip under the metal binder. The other three sides should be 1/4 inch smaller than the size of the album. See Figure A.

Round the two outside corners of each board. For the side that slips under the binder, score along the inside edge so the cardboard bends and the album will close when it is finished. See Figure A.

Remove cardboard inserts from the album. Lay one on top of the iron-on interfacing. Trace around the cardboard, making the tracing 1/2 inch larger on all sides. Cut the fabric the same size as the interfacing. Iron the interfacing to the fabric. Repeat this procedure for the other piece of cardboard.

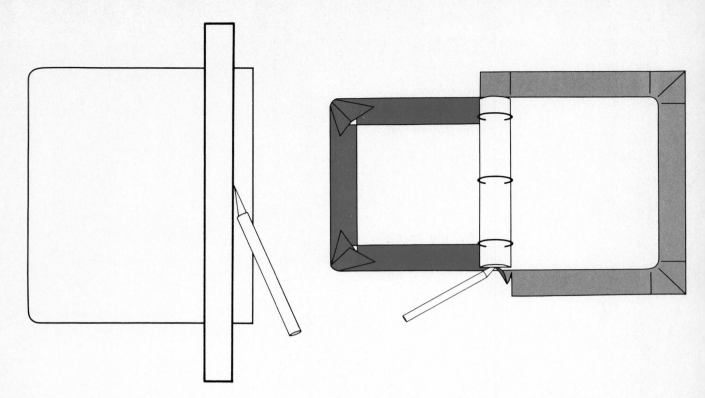

Figure A—Use ruler as guide. Score 1/2 inch from edge by cutting into, but not through, cardboard. This forms a crease so the cardboard can be bent along the score line.

Figure B—Raw edges in binder area are concealed by sliding them under metal. Other raw edges are covered by cardboard inserts.

ASSEMBLY

Place the open album face down on the work area. Spray the outside cover with adhesive. Lightly spray the facing side of the larger piece of fabric.

When adhesive on the outside of the open album is tacky, see page 13, set batting on top of it. Lay the large piece of fabric, facing-side up, on a clean surface. Center the open album on top of the facing, so batting is sandwiched between it and the album.

Trim the large piece of fabric around the album to 2 inches wide on all edges. Spread a thin layer of glue around the edges of the inside cover. Pull fabric tightly over these edges, and press firmly into the glue.

For corners, cut into the fabric 1/8 inch from the album. Trim this cut area in a curve. Pull the fabric over the edges, and press firmly into the glue. See Figure B. For the binder area, cut into fabric 1/8 inch from the album on either side of the binder. See Figure B. With a utility knife or blade, gently slide the fabric under the binder.

Set the album aside, and begin working on the cardboard inserts. Lay both inserts down on the work area, along with cut fabric fused with interfacing. Lightly spray one side of each card-board piece and the facing side of the material. Center the cardboard over the facing, tacky sides together. Press in place with fingers.

Fold over and glue the raw edges to the wrong-side of the cardboard. This is done the same way the raw edges were pulled to the inside cover of the album. Clip and curve the corners as shown in Figure B.

Before gluing inserts in place, measure the amount of lace needed to go around the album edge. Set the lace aside. Put glue on the inside cover of the album and the wrong-sides of the cardboard inserts. Position inserts on each side of the cover. Slide the long inside edge directly under the binder. Position the scored edge of the cardboard in the fold of the album.

Find the center of the lace so when it is applied, edges will meet at the metal binder. At the top of the album, place lace between the cardboard and album. Work around the edges until all the lace is added. Lace can be slipped under the metal binder. Clamp the glued areas in position until glue dries.

Place the covered frame on the album and glue in place. Set heavy books on top until glue dries. To cover frames, see page 152.

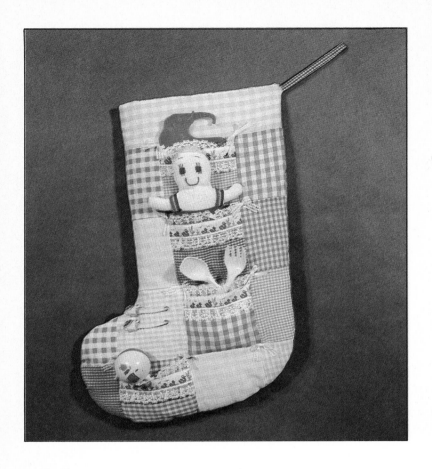

Gift Stocking

Squares are machine-sewn and quilting is done with simple ties. Your sock can be made in checks, dots, calico or traditional Christmas fabrics.

EQUIPMENT
- **Scissors, page 20**
- **Sewing supplies**

MATERIALS
- **30 pieces of woven, washable fabric, 4-1/4 inches square**
- **3/8 yard of thin quilt batting**
- **3/8 yard of interfacing**
- **3/8 yard of 45-inch-wide fabric for lining**
- **1/8 yard of 45-inch-wide fabric for cuff**
- **1/2 yard of trim**

PIECING FRONT AND BACK OF SOCK

Enlarge the pattern, using the technique described on page 12. Cut out the pattern pieces according to the pattern shown in Figure A. For a template, cut a 4-1/2-inch square. See page 15.

Sock Front—Cut 30 pieces that are 4-1/4 inches square. Choose four squares to be used for pockets. On each pocket, fold the raw edges under 1/4 inch and press. Fold under 1/4 inch again, press and machine- or hand-stitch. Sew trim across the top of each pocket from edge to edge. Pin each pocket to a square. Match edges on the bottom and sides.

Use 14 squares for the sock front. Arrange them as shown in Figure B. To make the first row, sew three squares together along the side edges with a 1/4-inch seam. Press each seam to the darker fabric.

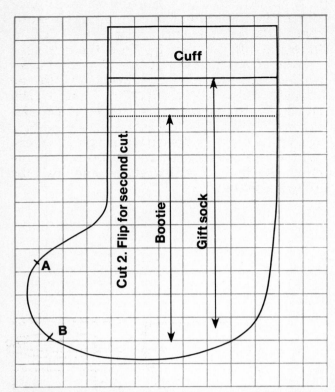

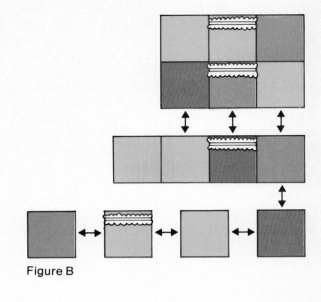

Each square equals 1 inch.

Figure A—The solid line at the top indicates the cuff. The dotted line indicates the pattern for the *Texture Sock*, page 147. Mark pattern *Front* and *Back*. For lining and piecing, cut one *Front*, then turn pattern over and cut one *Back*.

Proceed in the same manner with the second, third and fourth rows. To sew the rows together, put the second row on top of the first, with right-sides together. Match the raw edges, and pin at the seams. Stitch the long bottom edge with a 1/4-inch seam. See page 15 for more information on piecing.

With right-sides together and raw edges matching, pin and sew the third row to the second. Sew the fourth row to the third in the same manner. When piecing is complete, iron seams toward the darker fabric.

Cut a sock front from the pieced material. Do *not* cut a cuff. Lay the material on a surface, right-side up. Place the pattern on top of the fabric so squares for pockets are centered. Pin, trace around the pattern with pencil or other marker, then cut out the piece.

To make a cuff, cut fabric according to the pattern. See Figure A. With right-sides together and raw edges even, pin the cuff to the top of the sock. Stitch along the raw edge 1/4 inch from the edge. See Figure C.

Sock Back—Before sewing squares together, lay them on the pattern in the reverse order of the sock front. If the top row of the sock front is orange, blue and green, the top row of sock back will be green, blue and orange. Sew the seam the same way as the sock front, with or without pockets. Flip the pattern over to make a sock back. See Figure A.

PUTTING SOCK TOGETHER

Cut batting the size of the sock with the cuff. See Figure A. Cut a piece of interfacing larger than the sock. Put the sock front or back on top of the batting. Place the batting on top of the interfacing, and baste the three layers together.

Tie each corner of the pieced squares through all thicknesses, page 19. When tying is complete, cut the interfacing to match the shape of the sock.

With right-sides facing, pin together the quilted back and front pieces. Baste the sock together, adding a loop for hanging on the back of the sock at the cuff. See Figure D. If necessary, trim edges of the interfacing and batting to match the sock front and back. Sew 1/4 inch from all raw edges, except the top. Turn right-side out, and remove basting-stitches.

To make the lining, cut two pieces of fabric from the larger version of the pattern, which includes the cuff. Cut one piece from the sock front and one from the sock back. Pin right-sides together, and stitch around all edges, except the top and toe. See Points A and B in Figure A. Slip the lining over the sock, with right-sides together. Match raw edges at the cuffs. Sew around the edges of the cuffs through all layers. Pull the sock out through the toe opening of the lining. Stitch the opening closed and stuff the lining inside the sock.

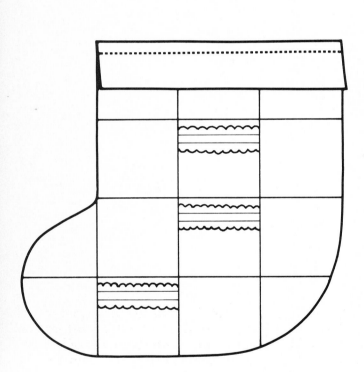

Figure C

Figure D—Place loop inside socks, with raw edges matching. See page 18 for making loops.

Bibliography

Sewing Books

Complete Guide to Sewing. Pleasantville, N.Y.: Reader's Digest, 1976.

Sewing, The Complete Guide. Tucson: HPBooks, Fisher Publishing, Inc., 1983.

The Complete Family Sewing Book. New York: Playmore, Inc. Publishers, 1980.

Vogue Sewing. New York: Harper & Row Publishers, 1982.

Craft Books

Margaret Boyd. *Catalog Sources for Creative People*. Tucson: HPBooks, Fisher Publishing Inc., 1981.

Barbara Brabec. *Creative Cash*. Tucson: HPBooks, Fisher Publishing Inc., 1981.

Maria DiValentin. *Practical Encyclopedia of Crafts*. New York: Sterling Publishing Co., Inc., 1970.

Dan Munson & Allianora Rosse. *The Paper Book: 187 Things to Make*. New York: Charles Scribner's Sons, 1970.

Mary Walker Phillips. *Step-By-Step Macrame*. New York: Golden Press, 1970.

Ed Reinhardt & Hal Rogers. *How to Make Your Own Picture Frames*. New York: Watson-Guptil Publishers, 1966.

Barbara Stephan. *Creating with Tissue Paper*. New York: Crown Publishers, Inc., 1973.

Ruth Thomson. *Exciting Things to Make in Paper*. New York: J. B. Lippincott Co., 1977.

Gloria Vanderbilt. *Book of Collage*. New York: Galahad Books, 1970.

Sewing and Hand-Craft Books

Joan Fisher. *Guide to Embroidery*. London: Trewin Copplestone Publishing Ltd., 1973.

Julie Houston, ed. *Woman's Day Book of Best-Loved Toys & Dolls*. New York: Sedgewood Press, 1982.

Mollie Mordle-Barns. *Making Children's Clothes*. New York: Good Housekeeping Books, 1977.

Grete Peterson & Elsie Svennas. *Handbook of Stitches*. New York: Van Nostrand Reinhold Company, 1970.

Phyllis Schwabke & Margery Dorfmeister. *Sewing with the New Knits*. New York: MacMillan Publishing Co., Inc., 1975.

Susan Warten, ed. *How To Make Soft Toys & Dolls*. Menlo Park, CA.: Lane Publishing Co., 1977.

Quilting

Alyson Smith Consalves, ed. *Quilting & Patchwork*. Menlo Park, CA.: Lane Publishing Co., 1975.

Barbara G. Jackson. *Patchwork Quilts*. New York: Playmore, Inc. Publishing, 1978.

Yvonne M. Khin. *Quilt Names & Patterns*. Washington, D.C.: Acropolis Books, Ltd., 1980.

Marjorie Puckett. *String Quilts & Things*. Orange, CA.: Orange Patchwork Publishers, 1979.

Index

Acknowledgments

Special thanks goes to Donna Sessions for her ideas, time and support. Thanks also to Marianna Dodson for her *Appliqued Quilts and Hangings*, Cynthia Johnoff for *Andrew's Primary Quilt* and Pamela Rhodes for her photo of the *Party Dress*.

The following people also contributed to the projects in this book: Karen Alongi, Opal Barnhart, Susan Beebe, Ellen Beimfohr, Vicki Lynn Gatzke, Patti George, Ramona Greene, Anne Hoffman, Christopher Nast, Richard Nast, Frances Stalcup, Margaret Thacker, Jeannie Wager and Verity Witzeman.

Additional thanks go to Robert Lebsack, Ron Sessions and the following models: Marcus Aaron Barnes-Cannon, Kurt Beimfohr, Kimberlee Elliot, Marques A. Elliot, Vicki Lynn Gatzke, Kimberley Renae Greene, Tyson Hudgel, Garret Husted, Melinda Lebsack, Salina May Locke, Andrew Meyer, Andrew Nast, Christopher Nast, Lindsay Price, Leigh Anne Sessions, Veronica Valenzuela and Tyler Jean Wager.